Jason Webster was born in S… … …
up in England and Germany. …
Oxford and living for several years in Italy and Egypt, he
went to Spain to learn to play the flamenco guitar …

the … … … …

… … …

'An eloquent eulogy on the richness of the cultural life in Moorish Spain . . . An assured blend of travel and history that informs, persuades and diverts in equal measure. Webster's evident passion for his subject makes this essential reading for anyone who has even heard of Spain' *Waterstone's Books Quarterly*

'An Arabic odyssey through Iberia . . . Like *Duende*, Webster's highly regarded flamenco-centred debut, there's no doubting the author's passion for his subject' *Wanderlust*

'*Andalus* gives a thought-provoking insight into the Moorish footprints still evident in modern Spain and provides a fresh perspective on both the current political climate and age-old traditions' *A Place In The Sun*

'Webster's examination of the relationship between Spain and Islamic culture is timely and gripping' *Living Spain*

Acclaim for *Duende*:

'Webster quickly discovers the *compás*, or rhythm, of his narrative voice; the result is a compelling account of a culture closed to most *guiris* (foreigners) and infinitely darker and more dramatic than the colourful tourist spectacles would have them believe . . . Webster has skilfully edited his experiences . . . he resists the temptation to go into too many descriptive flights about the Spanish landscape, instead creating a sense of place through the conversations of the characters he meets and their immediate environments . . . he has a talent for finding moments of humour in unlikely places without overplaying them. Perhaps his greatest achievement is to involve the reader so deeply in the narrator's diffuse quest that what the potential to be a fairly self-indulgent memoir instead becomes a page-turner. *Duende* is an intensely personal portrait of a country in the throes of modernisation, whose spirit still defies definition' *Observer*

'Ever wanted to run away and join the gypsies? Don't. That way lies heartache, flame-haired temptresses (married, with gun-toting husbands and knife-wielding lovers) and lines of white powder laid on the bonnets of stolen BMWs at dawn. Hooked? You will be. If there's such a thing as literary *duende* – the word used in flamenco for what happens when everything goes right – Jason Webster has it in spades . . . it's unputdownable. The autobiography-as-travelogue that is also a rite of passage is a form which worked brilliantly for

Laurie Lee and Bruce Chatwin – both novelists as well as seekers after the truth-behind-the-truth. Ladies and gentlemen, we have a new star of the genre: James Webster' *Daily Mail*

'*Duende* is a fascinating book, the most gripping I have read for years. I can't remember ever before having stuck my fingers in my ears to block out the wails of my children in order to finish a chapter.

The best travel writing is not about topography but people, and Webster's infiltration of this notoriously closed community makes for compulsive reading. Spain is so often described as a colourful place, but Webster does justice to the greys and blacks of it too: the street-corner junkies, the miserable flats, the lack of imagination. It's not all about driving over lemons.

The greatest strength of the book may be that it mimics, in its own structure, Webster's quest for duende. At the beginning the writing is as uncertain as the writer, but it gathers confidence and pace until, by the middle section, which deals with Madrid, it is exhilarating. This is the moment of hair-raising, spine-tingling, child-ignoring duende.

I know from my own experience living among Madrid's trans-vestites, poets and revolutionaries that Spain is the strangest place. It is disconcertingly easy to cross a line there and find your-self embroiled in events that seem bizarre when examined in the cold light of day ... Jason Webster is an exceptional writer, and this is a great book' *Guardian*

'Here, flamenco is shown to stand for all that is wild, anti-establishment and passionate in Spain. It is, in Carmen's words, a bohemian child. This is a romantic view ... one that quickly seduces our traveller and us with him. For a first book, indeed for any book, Webster's writing has great assurance, and there are some superbly constructed moments ... an impressive début ... *Duende* sweeps along from one harmonious chord to the next and builds into a crescendo that is as rich in atmosphere and emotion as the world it seeks to portray ... what it does most successfully is describe a young man's rite of passage through a foreign culture, a journey from which he emerges with a greater understanding of his subject and considerably wiser about the nature of human relationships ... passionate and evocative' *Sunday Times*

'*Duende* is indefinable, (a know-it-when-you-experience-it thing), but it is when everything comes together perfectly. Luis Antonio de Vega said, "Flamenco is the means through which man reaches God without the intervention of the saints or angels". Real flamenco is exciting, alive, vibrant, and above all, passionate.

Alive, vibrant and passionate are good words to describe Jason Webster's outstanding début book ... *Duende* is the most authentic and compelling account of flamenco in English, and one of the best books ever written about Spain' *Literary Review*

'Webster's Spain is remorselessly modern, urban and inhabited not merely by the standard *picaros gitanos* and colourful low-life of the traditional Hispanophile's lexicon, but also tourists, foreign residents and the Costa tackiness which J.G. Ballard evoked so effectively in his recent *Cocaine Nights* ... thirty years ago this book would undoubtedly have been written as a first novel; it has the pace, crisp dialogue and narrative drama which characterized a certain type of male, heterosexual Anglo-Saxon fiction. The traditions of the Bildungsroman and the rites-of-passage novel have migrated into the travel genre' *Times Literary Supplement*

'Webster ... has an exquisite nose for trouble, and it is the diversions on the road to flamenco that make such enjoyable reading ... the mix of romance and determination that propels Webster through life is more than enough to bring the reader along too' *Irish Times*

'Webster became obsessed with *duende* while studying at Oxford, heading to Spain on graduation to learn flamenco guitar and find out more.

Underscoring this search is a more personal journey; the desire to slough off a lingering immaturity and transcend the emotionally repressed make-up of the typical Englishman through immersion in a culture more attuned to passion and its expression. The two themes – the search for *duende* and the search for self – harmonise perfectly.

Webster's experiences are skilfully edited and neatly shaped too, the selective dramatisations and insights into character lending the book the feel of a novel. In its unassuming way it contains multitudes – a young man's emotional growth, a history of flamenco, and a view of a very different Spain to the one we're accustomed to reading about and visiting. Music, passion, drugs, a "beakerful of the warm South" – who could resist all that in these dark days?' *Time Out*

Also by Jason Webster

DUENDE: A Journey in Search of Flamenco

and published by Black Swan

Andalus

Unlocking the Secrets of
Moorish Spain

Jason Webster

BLACK SWAN

ANDALUS
A BLACK SWAN BOOK : 9780552771245

Originally published in Great Britain by Doubleday,
a division of Transworld Publishers

PRINTING HISTORY
Doubleday edition published 2004
Black Swan edition published 2005

3 5 7 9 10 8 6 4 2

Set in 11/13pt Melior by
Falcon Oast Graphic Art Ltd.

Black Swan Books are published by Transworld Publishers,
61–63 Uxbridge Road, London W5 5SA,
a division of The Random House Group Ltd.

Addresses for Random House Group Ltd companies outside the UK
can be found at: www.randomhouse.co.uk
The Random House Group Ltd Reg. No. 954009.

Printed and bound in Great Britain by
Cox & Wyman Ltd, Reading, Berkshire.

The Random House Group Limited supports The Forest Stewardship
Council (FSC), the leading international forest certification organisation.
All our titles that are printed on Greenpeace approved FSC certified paper
carry the FSC logo. Our paper procurement policy can be found at:
www.rbooks.co.uk/environment.

Mixed Sources
Product group from well-managed
forests and other controlled sources
www.fsc.org Cert no. TT-COC-2139
© 1996 Forest Stewardship Council

For Pepe, Zine el Abedine B. and Lucía F. S.

ما ليتكلم فى ألكركاع غير ألخاوي //

CONTENTS

ACKNOWLEDGEMENTS

I would like to thank the following people for their help with this book:

José and Maribel Valdivia; Emilio Galindo; Dr Robin Ostle; Alan Jones; Dr Jeremy Johns; Jessica Hallett; Conceiçao Amaral; Belén D'Souza; Santiago Macias; Fernando Tuvilla; Esther Lieft; HRH Prince José-María de Almuzara y Navarro; Miles Roddis; Juan Ferzerode; Muhammad López; Faelo; Amadeo García; Sayed Arash and Hazel Debestani; Shaykh Ziyendi; Salma Grimwood; Kifah Arif; Oriental Institute, University of Oxford.

My agent, Natasha Fairweather, has been a constant support, patiently putting up with my crazier ideas until the right one came along. Emma Parry in New York also gave very useful advice at the start. Everyone at Transworld has been superb, particularly Marianne Velmans, Diana Beaumont and Kate Samano. Very special thanks go to my editor Sarah Westcott for her invaluable contribution.

And, of course, to Salud. *Con todo mi amor.*

Spain, first civilised by the Phoenicians and long possessed by the Moors, has indelibly retained the original impressions. Test her, therefore, and her natives by an Oriental standard.

Richard Ford, *A Handbook for Travellers in Spain*

Travel, and you will see the meaning of things.

Moroccan proverb

THE FARM

'If they catch you they will break your legs. You must leave at once.'

The old man looked away and moved as if to return to work. His thin dark skin glistened under a fur of grey whiskers and his purple lips were cracked and bloody from where he bit them and licked the scab with a circular motion of his tongue. His hands, bloated and hard, were stained pink from the endless fruit he had picked over the course of the season. How many dozens of oranges, strawberries, *nisperos* and lemons I'd eaten had been plucked by this man, I wondered.

The heat under the sheeting was tremendous. We were in a tunnelled underworld stretching for acres over the landscape: a gigantic flat greenhouse made of plastic designed to produce fruit at all times of the year. It was the only way to make things grow in this area – a toe-grip of the Sahara in Europe. This part of Spain was dry, but conditions, they said, were worsening. One day not even the plastic and the artificial conditions would be able to prevent it from becoming real desert. In the meantime the farmers were determined to extract everything they

16

could from the soil using cheap immigrant labour.

I had only been under the plastic for twenty minutes and I was already feeling faint – at an extremely humid thirty-nine degrees it felt as though there was barely enough air passing into my lungs to keep me alive. The light, steady and blinding, seemed to radiate from every surface, while the smell of labouring bodies blended with the sharp sweet scent of the fruit, producing a sickly, sweaty cocktail. But these men, of all ages, from youngsters in their late teens to the old Moroccan in front of me, worked nine, ten hours a day like this. And the little pay they got – if they got any at all – depended on how many boxes they could pack. Some could do as many as eighty-five or ninety in a day. But they were usually the lucky ones – people treated well and given proper contracts, with perhaps even a home to go to – Russians or Eastern Europeans. These men, all Moroccans, were less fortunate.

'I paid five thousand euros to get here,' one of them told me. 'I've been working three months now and they haven't given me anything.'

We spoke in a combination of Spanish, French and Arabic, making ourselves understood as best we could. Their grasp of the European languages was limited, while my Egyptian-dialect Arabic was strange and only partially intelligible to North African ears. I pushed the sweat away as it streamed into my eyes. I wasn't sure how much longer I could stay under here, trapped in this surreal white world, where the arched wooden ribs that held up the sheeting were the only breaks in the monotony of a plastic sky just inches above our heads.

'They keep us locked up at night. We can't get out. I haven't spoken to my family for weeks.'

Slavery was alive and well here. These men had been duped into working in Spain, tempted by the chance to earn money in Europe and perhaps make better lives for themselves. But instead some mafia-style organization had smuggled them over and forced them to labour in barely human conditions for no pay. They were underfed, confused and frightened.

'This place is dangerous,' the old man repeated, speaking in the high sing-song voice typical of North Africans. There was an increasing nervousness about him and the others gathered around. 'You must leave.'

He lifted himself from the crouching position we had adopted by the low metal rack used for supporting the fruit boxes. His dark-brown trousers were stained and dirty, frayed around the bottom. His ill-fitting shoes slipped up and down as he walked away. Some of the others who had gathered around made to move with him. It was too risky; fear overcame their curiosity in the foreigner who had suddenly appeared among them. I began to wonder if coming here had been such a good plan after all.

A few days earlier, I had spoken to my journalist friend Eduardo about the idea that had been pre-occupying me for some time.

'The Arabs in Spain?' he said.

'Not only the history,' I replied. 'What about now? Moors and Christians used to get on fine, but look at Moroccans and Spaniards today. It's a different story.'

I knew I could rely on Eduardo to give me interesting leads. He was the kind of journalist who always knew much more than he could ever write about – plenty of stories were kept out of the newspapers for fear of libel, or because of the proprietor's political connections.

'I'll tell you where you'll find the real thing. It's a scandal.'

He listed the farms along the coast where Moroccans and other North Africans were forced to work like slaves.

'Slaves?'

'They can't go to the police because they're here illegally and would just get sent straight back to Morocco,' he said. 'It's time you opened your eyes.'

'They're trapped, then.'

'It's not going to be easy getting in and out, son,' he said. 'We're talking mafia here. The farmers keep the workers under tight control. And they may well be armed. I've been wanting to break this story for months but my editor won't let me: says it's too risky. But don't worry – you'll be fine.'

And of course I jumped at the idea. I'd seen hundreds of North African immigrants in Spain – the area where I lived in Valencia had one of the highest concentrations in the country. And many, I knew, were here illegally, smuggled over the Strait of Gibraltar in fishing vessels or speed boats, or strapped underneath trucks crossing on the ferry from Ceuta or Tangier. The ancestors of these people had once ruled Spain – Al-Andalus, as they called it – but today they were as unwelcome as though the Reconquest had never ended. The Spanish didn't put them to the sword any more, but if caught they were quickly sent back over the water.

Eduardo's words echoed in my head as I watched these men melting in this plastic city, enslaved on a farm, picking plastic fruit for plastic supermarkets.

'Why have you come here?'

As the other Moroccans picked themselves up and

returned to work, one of them, a young man I guessed at being in his mid twenties, stayed behind, beckoning me with his hand to remain seated a moment. I hadn't noticed him before: in jeans and trainers, he was dressed like a typical young North African man in Spain. But his hair was longer than usual and he seemed less nervous than the others. He spoke better Spanish as well.

'I heard about the conditions here. I wanted to see if—'

'You're a journalist?'

'No.'

'Then why?'

I shrugged. 'I'm treasure hunting.'

'Here?' He smiled, his teeth brilliant white against his dark complexion. I noticed one of his teeth was set at an odd angle, slightly lower than the rest and pushed back, as though at some point he'd been punched incredibly hard. 'You've come to the right place,' he said with a laugh. 'This is a gold mine.'

He stuck his hands into the ground by his feet, breaking the hard dry shell on top to reveal clods of fresh brown earth underneath, unleashing a baked, musty odour into the air.

'ZINE!'

There was a rasping shout from behind. The other workers were shuffling as fast as they could in either direction away from us. The Moroccan skipped onto the balls of his feet and peered above the trenches of fruit lined along the tunnel. I turned to see where he was looking, dizziness flooding my head as I pulled myself up onto my knees. Through the plastic I could see three pairs of legs moving towards us, walking briskly and heavily through the sand-like soil on the other side of the sheeting. They spoke Spanish with strong southern accents.

I felt a slap on the back of my head, and with a thud my face hit the ground, the Moroccan's quivering hand holding me down.

'Jesus Christ!'

'Quiet!' he said.

'I can't breathe.' My nose was buried in the dirt; lumps of grit flew into my mouth with each breath, a bitter, cloying taste on my tongue. I wriggled to get free, but he held me down harder.

'Quiet! They're coming.'

With a twisting motion, I managed to pull my head loose and looked up. The Moroccan stared hard at me with bulging eyes. These farmers were dangerous; the old man had said so. If they found me, I would be in trouble. But despite the warnings I'd been given – even by Eduardo, who usually had a cavalier approach to entering 'forbidden' areas – I was still unaware of quite how much danger I was in. At most they'd throw me off the farm, I thought – nothing more.

But when I saw one of the farmers carrying a heavy stick, I began to wonder. Through the plastic it was hard to make out properly, but it looked suspiciously like a baseball bat.

There was a moment of silence. The men stopped just beside us on the other side of the sheeting and the two of us remained motionless, hunted animals not certain yet if they'd been trapped or still had a chance of escape. I wasn't sure how much they could see through the sheeting. Perhaps, I thought with mindless optimism, we could bluff our way out of this. My heart pushed its way upwards through my ribcage, cold passing through my stomach. The dizziness of earlier, I noticed, had gone.

It became clear, though, that the farmers were being led to where we were. A fourth person standing behind them pointed to the exact spot where we were crouching, and, veiled behind the white sheets, the three of them took a simultaneous step in our direction.

With a scooping movement, the Moroccan grabbed me by the armpit and hauled me to my feet; within a second we were running like gazelles along the tunnel, heads bent to avoid crashing into the low ceiling, all effort thrown into forward motion.

'¡AQUI! ¡AQUI!'

The farmers' shouts came hurtling after us. I had no idea how fast they could run. If we were lucky they'd be middle aged and well fed, unable to keep up with our younger legs. But we were trapped inside the tunnel: we would have to get out somewhere. How many entrances did these things have? Would we have to rip ourselves out of this cocoon and make a break for it across the fields? The few passageways outside the plastic were equally long and thin – if they found us there it would be like being caught in a firing range. I followed my companion blindly, my only hope.

'He's got a Moroccan with him. *Están bajando.* They're heading downhill.'

It was hard to make out which way the slope went as we powered past the fruit bushes, other workers pulling themselves out of the way as we sped past. The Moroccan was quick, his head steady above skinny hunched shoulders. For a moment I wanted to call out to ask where we were going, but if they heard our voices we would give ourselves away. Not that it mattered. The shouting around us would tell them where we were.

We ran faster, taking short shallow breaths, adrenaline feeding a belief that we were going to make it, that somewhere further along there would be a way out of this tunnel.

The Moroccan jerked to the right, ducking his head, and I saw him vanish through a plastic flap into the outside world. Without a thought I followed him through, into the sun on the other side. My lungs clawed at the fresher air. A quick check and I saw there was no one around, but immediately we were running again, turning to the left and heading down the passageway between one tunnel and the next, ahead of us nothing but more plastic – a dense ocean of white, with distant hilltops the only sign of land. I could breathe better here, but already my legs were losing strength, my heart straining to perform.

We reached the end of the passageway – a kind of junction with a main corridor that linked various gaps in the plastic. I thought we'd stop and look before crossing, but the Moroccan just kept running. He should know, I thought. But as we passed from one pathway to another, we came face to face with one of the farmers – a short man with no neck, shoulders like a bull and a dull inhuman look in his eyes. He held a baseball bat in his hands.

'*Vale*,' he said. And without any warning he brought the bat crashing down onto my lower left leg. Had I not managed to lift and turn it slightly before the impact, he might have broken my shin, but the blow was directed onto the calf muscle.

I doubled forward with shock, half falling to the ground, trying to keep myself upright to avoid a strike

23

on the back of my head. I lifted my arm in an instinctive attempt to ward him off, stumbling to shift my weight onto my right foot. The pain was immense. For a second I thought I might throw up.

There was a loud grunt and a groan; from the corner of my eye I saw the Moroccan throw his bony-framed body at the farmer, his hand grasping to get a grip around the man's neck before he could hit me a second time. The two of them toppled over, the bat falling to one side. The farmer thrashed wildly, but round and overweight, he was like an upturned beetle, his short arms vainly punching the air while the Moroccan sat on his chest and began heaving his head up and down on the ground, trying to knock him out. Dust rose up from the dry earth in a cloud as the two of them grappled with each other. The farmer's face was turning a thick shade of red.

'Stop,' I said, coughing in the haze.

'Run!' he shouted. 'Straight down there. Go!'

I didn't move. Through the panic and pain, a more rational voice was making itself heard inside me.

'¡Corre! The others are coming.' The Moroccan began punching at the farmer's throat.

Someone, I thought, was going to die here if I did as he said. Either he would kill the farmer or the others would kill him once they found him. The man had saved me: I wasn't about to run away. Besides, I wasn't sure if I'd be able to.

'Run!'

The farmer's head was flopping about and his arms had stopped trying to hit up at his assailant. For a second I thought he was unconscious before I saw his eyes were still open. He looked as if he had concussion.

24

'Get off him,' I said. And limping over, I pulled the Moroccan off the prostrate farmer.

'*¿Estás loco?* Are you mad?'

'Grab that stick,' I said. He walked over to where the farmer's weapon lay on the ground and made as though to hit him over the head with it.

'No!' I held out my arm. The farmer began to groan like a child, incomprehensible words tumbling from his half-open mouth. Perhaps it was the pain in my leg, or seeing him so helpless, but I was unable to feel anger towards him. All thoughts were of escape and the other farmers.

'Here.' Stumbling, I went to lift the man up. 'We'll leave him in this passageway.' Then, turning to the Moroccan, 'Come with me.'

We dragged the farmer to the side, propping his head up against the plastic wall of one of the tunnels. He looked all right, just shaken and bruised. But we had to move fast. The others would find him soon. Already the workers inside were beginning to shout about the fight: news of what was happening was spreading like ink.

We began running again, down the hill. I willed myself forwards, my left leg reluctantly forced to work as the muscles clenched with pain, hopping and skipping my way behind the Moroccan. The old man had been right – they were a violent lot. I didn't want to find out what would happen if they caught us now.

In the distance behind us I could hear dogs barking. I'd seen Spanish farm dogs before – notoriously ferocious creatures that often killed one another in fights to the death. If they were loose, they would rip our throats out.

'Go!' I shouted ahead. 'Faster.'

25

I didn't care about the other farmers any more. The dogs had put the fear of God in me. I desperately wanted to get out of there.

'Down here.' The Moroccan weaved to the right and I sprinted after him, all thoughts about my leg evaporating with fear. Ahead, two hundred yards in front of us, there was a break in the whiteness – a little brown streak, barely a smudge, but the first sign of an end to the labyrinth – a dirt track, leading somewhere, anywhere, it didn't matter.

Emerging from the plastic world, we burst out onto the road. There was nothing in sight – no nearby town, no traffic, no immediate way to escape from the murderous farmers working their way towards us. I stopped, half choking as my lungs tightened with exhaustion, black spots flashing before my eyes. Where should we go? We had to keep running. But left or right?

Before I could decide, the Moroccan had grabbed my arm again and was hauling me up the hill. I couldn't believe what he was doing. We could at least keep following the slope downwards to make things easier for us. But he seemed certain of where he was going. My head was bent down as we ran, shoulders sloping forwards, and I clutched at the stitch now stinging in my side. Briefly I looked up and saw ahead of us a dirty red Derbi moped parked in the shade beneath a eucalyptus tree, a helmet balanced on the back seat.

'I just hope we can get it started,' I thought.

In a few more paces we had reached the bike. I looked back: there was no sign of our pursuers, but the dog-barking was still there, like creeping black ice.

'Get on.' The Moroccan was already gripping the handlebars: the key had been left in the lock and he was pumping at the pedals to get the tiny motor running. With a last effort I pushed the helmet to the ground and seated myself behind him, trying not to fall off as we jumped off the stabilizers and the back wheel touched the ground. The motor screamed as we headed down the hill, back towards the point where we had come out from the farmland. If they found us it would almost certainly be now. I stared ahead, eyes fixed on the gap in the plastic from which they would emerge.

We couldn't hear the barking now for the complaining high-pitched wail of the bike: there was no way of telling how close they might be. But they would have heard us, and would be moving in fast. I kept my eyes fixed on the gap: outrunning their dogs on this thing would not be easy.

With the slope working in our favour, we gained momentum as we moved closer and closer to the moment when we would know whether or not we had made good our escape. As the Moroccan pulled harder on the accelerator, the tunnel moved into focus. Then in a second it flashed by and we had gone past, leaving my mind with the clear photo-image of two farmers stumbling towards the track. No dogs with them, but one of them, I was sure, had been holding a handgun.

'Faster.' I squeezed the Moroccan's arm; the bike barely responded.

I looked behind me to where the two men would now appear. It was not far to the first corner in the road – once we reached it we would be out of range. But if they got to us before then? 'Pistols are useless over more than twenty or thirty yards,' a soldier friend had once told me. 'There's no accuracy there.' At least if he fired at us there was a high chance of him missing.

Lifting myself to see above the Moroccan's shoulder, I could see we were still about twenty seconds away from safety.

In my mind's eye I had already seen the image before I turned round again. The two men were there, standing still now having run out onto the road, one resting on his stick, the other raising his arm, the black metal weapon held firm in his outstretched hand. 'He's going to fire at us,' I thought. 'The bastard's going to shoot us.' I found myself ducking instinctively, as though to make a smaller target, still turned backwards to stare at our would-be assassin. Do you actually see the bullets, I wondered. A flash, perhaps.

I never found out. The Moroccan suddenly threw one arm out to hold onto me as he jerked the bike sharply to the left, along a track that forked off down the hill and away from view. The plastic city vanished behind the crest of the slope, and with it the two farmers, the pistol, the dogs, the danger. They wouldn't follow us now. We were safe.

MUSA THE MOOR

*C*himo claimed he never liked the shape of his nose anyway, and that if he were twenty years younger he would emigrate. He couldn't understand why I lived in Spain. The place was going from bad to worse, and these *populares* had been in power for too long now.

'This violence is their fault, and just the beginning,' he said, still dabbing spots of blood with a handkerchief. But then England, he admitted with a sigh, had also produced *La Thatcher* and *los hooligans*, and now *el señor Bush* was about to invade Iraq, so perhaps I was better off here after all.

Except that time was running out.

I'd been going to see Chimo about once a fortnight for years, ambling down to his snug secondhand bookshop just a few streets away from my flat in Valencia, deliberately walking past the bigger, overpriced shop next door belonging to his fat, bald rival. Chimo would usually be sitting behind his scratched wooden desk, flicking through dusty lingerie catalogues or simply staring through his square spectacles at a street half screened out by the rarely sold books he placed on display. Opposite was a Moroccan grocer's, while the bar next door was run by Algerians. Immigrants had concentrated in this part of the city: North Africans, Ecuadoreans and Chinese.

Chimo would offer me a cigarette, and with a slight weariness in his voice ask what kind of thing I was looking for: times were tough, and I was expected to be part of the solution; you felt that even if you offered to buy his entire stock, it could never be enough, somehow. I'd pick something up on his recommendation, often a book I wasn't especially interested in – a novel from the 1950s about life on the France–Spain border, or a guide to rural architecture in Castilla-León – with the idea that it could come in useful at some point. I was sure that one day he would lift some gem from his grubby shelves and hand it to me with his nonchalant shrug, looking at me out of the corner of his grey eyes as if to say, 'Will he take the bait?'

'Have you seen what they're doing now?' he said that afternoon as soon as I walked into his shop. His wrinkled face looked puffed and swollen. 'Another billion on that new museum and they can't even come and fix the drains. A storm the other night and ¡hala! the stink! Smells like a sewerage farm here. And then those young fascists start coming round saying it's because of the *moros*, that there are too many of them, and they shit so much they're blocking up the pipes. It's a bloody joke. I told them, get out, I said. I don't want you lot round here. We didn't live through the dictatorship just to see people like you knocking on our doors . . . That's when he hit me.'

I looked at this skinny old man, spectacles bandaged together with sticky tape over his swollen and bruised nose, and felt a surge of anger towards the moron who'd done this to him. Things had been tense since

31

the anti-immigrationists had taken over a heavy-metal bar five doors down the road. Most of them worked as bouncers at various nightclubs around the city. The week before, two Moroccans had been knifed; the district was in danger of becoming a no-go area.

'Does it hurt?' I asked. He was a proud man, and I didn't want to push it too far.

'No. *¡Que va!* It's nothing.' He shrugged and lit a cigarette. 'It's only fractured.' He began leafing through some papers in a drawer to show how unaffected by it all he was.

'What these idiots don't understand,' he said, looking up, 'is the *moros* were here even before they were. Ha! Valencia was Moorish for centuries. These yobs don't read, that's their problem. If they did they'd know. Ruzafa, the name of this part of town, is Arabic: it means orchard, or garden, or something like that. These Moroccans have as much right to be here as anyone.'

His words struck a chord. I'd often thought that Spain had retained more of its 'Moorishness' than people cared to admit. Arabs and Berbers had lived here for almost nine centuries, and sometimes, looking at ordinary 'Spanish' faces, it seemed they had never left. The Alhambra in Granada, the Great Mosque in Córdoba – these were beautiful and dramatic reminders of the Islamic civilization that had once flourished in Spain. But it seemed likely that its legacy ran deeper than a few ancient buildings and a collection in a museum – nine hundred years was a long time. There were moments when you could sense some lingering *Thousand and One Nights* magic about the place: exoticism, but perhaps something more than that as well: a world man had yet to throw out of balance by believing he could impose his will with impunity on fate and nature. I found constant echoes from the time I'd spent living in the Middle East – in the food, the people, the buildings and the customs.

'I shit on the whore! You think this is a democracy? Well, you're wrong. Time is running out. These skinheads will be in power one day soon, just like the fascists before them. Under Franco you couldn't even see two people kissing in a film. That's right – they'd cut it just before their lips met. Now, if I want to, I can go down the nudist beach and see as much as I want, when I want. Don't know about you, not everyone's cup of tea, but it's the most natural thing in the world to feel the sun all over. And there are some beauties down there, too . . .'

Despite being in his late sixties and the latest victim of right-wing thuggery, you couldn't help feeling that some adolescent part of Chimo's imagination was still very active, and was probably thriving on his spending too much time alone in his little shop. It was an innocent form of lechery, though: he could be a perfect gentleman, as I'd seen on the odd occasion when women had walked in.

'Still treasure hunting?' he asked with a grin as I glanced momentarily back at the shelves. I was still angry about what had happened to him, but had heard him eulogize the female form often enough.

'Just like your predecessor, *el pirata Drake*.'

In Spain the great English hero – explorer, sea captain and bugbear of Philip II – was reduced to a mere 'pirate'.

'You lot always come to Spain looking for spoils,' he said. 'Take Gibraltar for a start.'

'That's not English: it's Moorish,' I said with a laugh.

'I know. Gibraltar – *jabal Tariq* – the mountain of Tariq, the first Arab to conquer Spain. He landed there before marching north.'

'The *first* Arab?' I asked vaguely.

'Before Musa came along. Musa was Tariq's boss. Came after Tariq and took all the glory. Created the greatest civilization on earth, the Moors did. Right here in Spain. We had the first universities, the first paper factories, the first street lighting in the whole of Europe.'

The Moors had first crossed the Strait of Gibraltar during the Dark Ages, at about the same time as Bede was writing his *History*, over half a century before the first Viking attacks on the Northumbrian coast. Muslim armies had recently spread out from the Arabian peninsula following the establishment of Islam and the death of the Prophet Muhammad, conquering as far as the Himalayas in the east and North Africa in the west. According to the old accounts, the Christian Count Julian of Ceuta, angry over the rape of his daughter by the Spanish King Roderic, asked the newly arrived Muslims to cross over into Spain to avenge him. Spain at that time was under Visigothic rule, the Germanic tribe having moved in and taken over as the Roman Empire collapsed.

In the year 711 a small Moorish force led by the commander Tariq crossed the Strait of Gibraltar. 'Moor' was the term often used to describe the Muslims in Spain – an ethnically diverse group comprising Arabs, Berbers, Syrians, Persians and eventually Spaniards themselves; it originated from the Latin *maurus*, which had been used to refer to

North Africans. It was a loose and fuzzy term, but often more accurate than simply 'Arab' or 'Muslim' – words that were usually too strict for the blurred divisions of the time. The following year a second group led by Musa also crossed over, and in a short period the two armies had taken control of most of Spain and started moving into France. At the Battle of Poitiers in 732, a hundred years after the Prophet Muhammad's death, the Muslims suffered defeat at the hands of the Franks and subsequently retreated behind the Pyrenees, more or less. This was the birth of 'Al-Andalus', what the Moors called the territory in Spain and Portugal they controlled. The name was of uncertain origin: some said it came from 'Vandal', as the migratory tribe had briefly crossed through Spain on their way to North Africa in the sixth century; others said it was a derivation of an old Visigothic word *landahlauts* – a territory divided up by lots; others that it was an Arabic mispronunciation of 'Atlantic', or 'Atlantis'.

Despite the Muslims' rapid success, there were small areas in the very north of Spain, around Asturias, that remained relatively untouched. At first they posed little problem for the new Moorish rulers, but centuries later they would become the starting points for various Christian campaigns southwards, in what eventually became known as the 'Reconquest'.

Although initially a distant outpost of the recently formed Islamic Empire, Al-Andalus soon became caught up in the internal divisions that broke out at the political centre. Following several violent conflicts over the leadership of the Muslim community – the caliphate – a group called the Abbasids swept aside the ruling Umayyads in 750, massacring almost the entire family at a feast. At least one member survived, however, and fled to the protection of his mother's Berber tribe in what is now Morocco. This man then crossed over to Al-Andalus, where he established himself as a new ruler, breaking away from the recently established power base in Baghdad. Abd al-Rahman I was thus the first effective emir of Moorish Spain. Religiously the country was still part of the Islamic world, yet politically it became independent.

The first two hundred years or so saw the gradual establishment of Moorish rule: the native population – a mixture mainly of Romano-Iberians, Celts, Jews and the former Visigothic rulers – began to take on the customs of their new masters, speaking Arabic and wearing Arab-style clothes. Bit by bit they started converting to Islam, although the pressure to do so was mainly financial – Christians and Jews were tolerated and protected, but had to pay a special tax. The conquering armies had been relatively small – perhaps just a few thousand – and intermarriage was common. As a result, the racial divide became very blurred. Soon afterwards, the same would happen on a cultural level: Muslims called Christians living in Al-Andalus *musta'rab* – 'would-be Arabs', *mozarabes* in modern Spanish. Sometimes it wasn't clear who were 'Arabs' and who were 'Spaniards'. Some historians preferred to describe Al-Andalus as the integration of Spain and Portugal into the Islamic world, rather than a military invasion and conquest by a foreign occupying force.

For most Spaniards, however, the Moorish period was little more than a brief and forgettable interlude in the country's past: Chimo's attitude was very unusual. School history books often talked about the Islamic period in a single chapter. The Moors were very much *them*, never *us*. Indeed, the concept of 'non-Moorishness' was a fundamental part of the Spanish national identity. The country's patron saint, St James or Santiago, was cheerfully given the nickname 'the Moor-slayer' for his supposed appearance in a number of battles against the Muslims. According to the orthodox view, almost as soon as the Moors had arrived the Reconquest began – a virtually continual process from the eighth century until the conquest of Granada in 1492. Since that date, the country and its culture had been Catholic and Latin-based and the Moors had been kept firmly on the other side of the sea. Today, annual 'Moors and Christians' fiestas, where the capture of a town for Christendom was painstakingly re-enacted, was for many the only real memory of the age of Al-Andalus.

It was a neat and simple story that masked the complexities of who the Spanish really were. In this view, the fall of Granada merely marked a return to the *status quo ante*.

'This is the scene of one of Christianity's finest hours,' a Granadino had once told me. 'From Asturias to Granada – a single reconquest campaign.'

A single campaign that lasted eight hundred years?

Imagine if the Sioux Nation rose up today, formed an alliance with other tribes, and at some point in the twenty-sixth century defeated the United States. Would their culture be purely 'Indian'? Would their final victory mark a return to how things were before the White Man took over? Those Indian reservations would swiftly be rewritten in the history books as unconquered lands – bastions of aboriginal civilization that withstood the onslaught and provided the launching pad for the subsequent reconquest of Indian territory. I had the feeling something very similar to this had happened in Spain.

'You know the folk tales about Musa the Moor.' Chimo continued with his history lesson. '"Watch out, or Musa the Moor will get you!" They say that to frighten kids. There are legends and all kinds of things about him. Here.'

And so it was that as he reached for a slim children's book behind him, with a simple drawing on the cover of a man in a turban holding his hand out towards a crescent moon, the moment I had always hoped for finally arrived: the book on Chimo's shelf that would open my eyes. *La Llegenda del Moro Mussa.*

'It's in Catalan,' I said worriedly, not realizing at first the importance of what he'd given me.

'Don't let that bother you. You'll understand. It's yours for three euros.'

Back at home, with the help of a dictionary, I began to read.

Musa the Moor was the richest, strongest and most powerful caliph who ever ruled in ancient Spain and he lived on top of a mountain in a luxurious palace with golden domed roofs and minarets that touched the sky. Seeing one day that Christian armies were advancing to conquer his lands, he decided to flee, but felt reluctant to leave his beautiful palace and all the riches he kept in it. In desperation, he pulled out a magic lantern he kept in a dusty cupboard, blowing on it until the jinn that lived inside came out and said in a sleepy voice, 'O Great Master! Your wish is my command.'

'O Wise Jinn,' the caliph said. 'Help me, please. I must save my treasure.' And he told the jinn about the advancing Christians.

'Do not fear, Noble Master,' the jinn said. 'All we must do is hide your riches from the eyes of the infidels by turning everything into stone. In that way they won't see them for what they truly are.'

'Good idea,' said Musa. 'Then make it so.'

But the Caliph's daughter, the Princess Zoraida, overheard the conversation, and she began to weep inconsolably when the jinn had left.

'Father,' she cried. 'I don't want to run away. I like this mountain, and the birds and flowers here, and the lovely perfumed air. Please, Father, let me stay.'

And so Musa the Moor ordered the jinn to place his riches – now turned into stone – in a special cave with a tree planted at the entrance. And that tree was his daughter, the Princess Zoraida, guarding her father's precious treasure.

All went well, but the jinn made one small mistake when casting his spell over the enchanted cave, so that on one day in every year, just as springtime is arriving, at midnight the Princess Zoraida comes back to life and all the Caliph's riches gleam and shine again. And the princess begins to spring-clean, singing while she polishes and dusts before once more the jewels turn into stone, and she must stand for another year guarding the cave.

And they say that only good children, if they are lucky enough, might hear her laughing as for one short day she is free to breathe the perfumed mountain air she loves so much.

I put the book down, the beginnings of a thought pushing its way to the surface.

Outside it was sunny, with the clawing heat of a late Mediterranean summer. Children in the nursery below my flat were waking up from their siesta and playful screams echoed around the block. Outside, a scrap collector and his wife crawled past in their truck, scanning the street for anything left lying around on the pavements. They stopped in front of my window and, ignoring the honking protests of the cars behind, got out and deftly hauled a discarded armchair into the back, where their two teenage boys wedged it securely between splintered wooden boards and old wardrobes. Just junk. I wouldn't have even noticed it otherwise. The truck drove off, the two boys fighting for a turn to sit in the new throne-like piece of furniture, their laughter rising above the growls of rage from the speed-obsessed car-drivers behind them.

There was much to be discovered, if only you knew how to open your eyes, I thought. How much else of the world around me was I failing to see? How many hundreds of treasures had I passed over, thinking of them merely as worthless stones?

The Musa legend began to uncurl before me, its message gradually becoming clear: there were probably all kinds of disguised legacies of the Arab period in Spain, many of them unknown and unrecognized. The Moors had hidden away jewels of a subtler kind, and the trick had been to make them appear like nothing very important at all. Finding them would require a new way of seeing.

It was time, I realized, to discover more about a country I still felt I barely knew but which, having fallen in love with a Spanish woman, I now called home. After living here on and off for ten years, I'd learnt something of its music and languages, yet in many ways it was still as foreign to me as it had ever been: a vast, complex land at once fascinating and reserved; open yet insecure about 'outsiders'. The key to understanding it now lay in my hands.

It was time to go in search of Musa's treasure.

THE PROMISE

*H*aving dumped the moped fifteen minutes after our escape, the Moroccan and I had found my car and were driving away along tarmacked roads, towns coming into view like oases of sanity amid the madness of the countryside. Advertising hoardings and flashing fizzy-drink signs dotted among the palm trees had a strangely comforting effect after being chased by violent slave-trade farmers. For some reason, it seemed less harm could come to us in a world where 'Nothing Washes Whiter'.

We reached the outskirts of the nearest city and stopped at a bar. The sun had gone behind hazy clouds, and a clamminess hung in the air. I ordered a couple of glasses of wine as we sat at a table by the window, guessing correctly that the Moroccan would have no problem with alcohol. We both needed a drink.

My calf muscle throbbed with a fuzzy ache. I lifted my trouser leg up to have a look – it was pink and swollen, with the first bluish signs of the heavy bruising that would come later. Broken blood capillaries made red, worm-like patterns over the skin. I prodded around it gently: it would be stiff for a while, but in a week or so I'd be fine. Still, I was annoyed with myself for not having foreseen the potential dangers of entering the farm. A certain timidness in me could sometimes give way to the complete opposite – a relaxed overconfidence bordering on the blasé. And as I'd been able to walk straight onto the farmland without encountering any resistance, I had become blind to the risk I was taking. If anyone saw me, I'd reasoned, they would probably take me for an East European immigrant, of which Eduardo had said there were plenty also working on the semi-legal farm. I could scarcely believe now how stupid I'd been not to have expected more security.

'I'm Jason,' I said to the Moroccan. We had hardly spoken in the car, and I was now feeling a bit calmer.

'Jasie,' he repeated. Like most Arabs, I noticed, he had a problem getting my name right. 'I'm Zine.'

He stretched out his arm and we shook hands. After what we'd been through it seemed an oddly formal thing to do. There was a kindness in his face, though, and his smiling brown eyes immediately made you feel he liked you.

'Did you find your treasure, then?' he asked.

His Spanish seemed fluent, accented with a stress on the 'd's like many Arabs, with a certain French influence in his vowel sounds.

I was still trying to take in what had happened, my mind in a state of semi-shock, and was not at all clear about what I should do next. I rubbed my leg and my eyes began to feel heavy as exhaustion set in. Amid the fog, though, was a growing and more pressing question: Zine had gained his freedom, but what would he do now?

The noise in the bar rose sharply as the TV was switched on and a row of middle-aged men on bar stools turned to watch a football match: it was half-time and the local side was losing one–nil. A grey-haired woman stood next to them with head-phones on, listening to the radio coverage and tutting loudly.

'*¡Hijos de la gran puta!* – Fucking arseholes!' she yelled through yellow teeth. No one paid her any notice.

I looked back at Zine. He was avoiding my gaze, pre-tending to concentrate on the replays of the foul that had cost the home side a penalty. The colours on the TV screen had been set high, so the little orange and white men running about on an acid-green back-ground looked more like cartoon characters than real people. In another corner of the room a second group of men were hunched over a table playing cards: *naipe*, they called them, a reminder of their Arabic origins – *naib*. The events of earlier seemed unreal.

'Don't worry about me,' Zine said with a smile, turn-ing away from the TV. Despite everything, I could sense a deep optimism in him, and an uncommon energy – I'd seen that during our escape. But obviously he was in a fairly desperate situation. He swallowed the last of his wine and I ordered some more.

'There's a proverb in Morocco,' he said. '*Al-umur mahdud wal-khawf alash* – Life has a limit so why be scared?'

I was slowly waking up to the fact that not only did I owe a debt of gratitude to this man – he'd got me out of one of the closest scrapes in my life – but also that he was now my responsibility. He had no work, no

46

papers and only the clothes he was standing in. All thanks to me.

'Why did you do that, anyway?' I asked him. 'You could have just disappeared like the others. You didn't have to run with me.'

'God knows,' he said, holding his palms out. 'This morning, I don't know why, I knew it would be my last day on the farm.'

'Do you have anywhere to go?' I asked. 'I could take you. Perhaps some friends or contacts somewhere.'

He turned back to the TV. If I had some obligation to him – and it was becoming ever clearer to me that I had – he was not going to hold me to it. The situation was as uncomfortable for him as it was for me.

From his silence, I realized he knew nobody in Spain. He'd been conned just like the rest of them at the farm, had probably paid some huge sum of money to be brought over, and now he had nothing.

'You need to work, right?'

He laughed and turned back to look me in the face. 'Of course I need work, but . . . On the farm I have work but no money. Now I have no work at all. Ha!' He chewed hungrily on the roast almonds the barman had left on the table for us.

There was a roar as the home team scored an equalizer. The men at the bar leapt off their stools and surged forward to get nearer the TV set, pushing into the table and spilling our drinks. The elderly woman with the radio headphones gave out a long nasal scream of joy, swinging her glass in the air above her head like a trophy. For a few minutes it was too loud for us to speak.

Zine cheered along with the others, although I was unsure quite how much he knew about local football.

It was more likely that he just wanted to blend in.

I should try to do something for him, perhaps find him a job somewhere, if I could. There were farms near Valencia where immigrants worked, but it was risky. Since the new law had been passed anyone found without the right documents was shipped out immediately, with no chance of appeal. But I couldn't just leave him here, even if he wanted me to. I was duty bound to sort things out. My father-in-law owned some orange groves. Perhaps he could help.

'Look,' I said. 'Come with me and I'll talk to people I know. I'll see what I can do. I'm sure . . .' I tailed off.

Someone changed the channel and images of armoured personnel carriers driving through the desert appeared on the screen. Large numbers of troops were arriving in the Gulf as preparations were made for a new war. The presenter spoke clearly and slowly about frantic diplomatic rows at the United Nations. Another clash in the cycle of conflict between Islam and the West was about to begin.

Zine smiled and looked down. He wanted to refuse, but this was the only opportunity he had.

It would be longer than I thought before the two of us went our separate ways.

THE ROAD TO
VALENCIA

'*T*hey said they'd kill us if we tried to escape. I didn't believe it – they were just trying to frighten us – but I stayed, waiting for the right moment. Jump too soon and you drown.'

Zine told me of his life on the farm as we sped towards Valencia, salt-white air blowing through our open windows as we neared the sea. The car had air conditioning, but every time I switched it on the engine temperature gauge crept perilously high, so we relied on the natural breeze – although in late summer this offered little relief.

'I've been there for over a year. There was no money in Morocco. They made us work like *perros*. No, worse than dogs. I have never seen dogs treated the way they treated us on that farm.'

Around us old Arab castles and watchtowers perched on pinnacles of yellow rock, their square-cut edges blending seamlessly with the jagged contours of the land. Down in the valley below sat the broken ruins of an abandoned farmhouse, like frayed threads in a crease of dark-brown fabric.

'We worked twelve hours a day or more, seven days

every week. Ten of us sleeping in a room. And all the time they're watching us to make sure we don't run away. Then every week we're told the money hasn't arrived, or we're damaging the crop so it can't be sold, so there's no money. Always holding back the money, always some excuse. The Algerians used to talk of killing them and escaping, but it was pointless. You kill them, you get away, they put you in prison or you end up dead. Either way there's no money. And they were armed. Most had knives, but one had a gun. I saw it: he made sure I did. Of course, they wanted us frightened. They wouldn't have used them in a fight. Not the gun.'

He paused, and for a moment I felt the weight of what he was telling me. If the authorities found him and discovered he was a *sin papeles* they would ship him off back to Morocco in less than forty-eight hours. He was placing himself in my hands: what would happen to him from here on depended largely on me. But what did he have to lose? Staying on at the farm was no better than taking his chances now.

'They're taking Poles and Romanians. No one wants *moros* any more. It wouldn't have taken them long to throw all of us out, drop us in front of the next Guardia patrol and watch us get sent back.'

In the distance the sea shone a sharp thick blue in the melting air, cars filing along the coast road like ants. A dusty pine fragrance circled inside the car, rising every once in a while on a wave of smothering Mediterranean heat.

'But I think things are changing for me, Jasie. I think this was the worst, you know? Things are going to be better from now on, *in sha' Allah* – God willing.'

We crossed the Júcar, the river whose sweet waters had inspired the Arabs to name it after one of their most popular imports to Spain: sugar, or *sukkar*; and passed into the ancient Moorish Kingdom of Valencia – Balansiya, as they had called it. The fertile market-gardening area around the city had barely changed since the Moors had developed the complex irrigation system that still watered it – the rice paddies and orange groves another horticultural legacy from those times. This was the Costa del Azahar – the Orange-Blossom Coast. *Azhar* in Arabic means 'flowers'.

'What's this trip about, Jasie?' Zine asked. 'A treasure hunt, you said.'

For a minute I just kept my eye on the road. I was a little reluctant to tell him too much, but at the same time I found myself opening up to him.

'I have this theory Spain is actually still a Moorish country,' I said. 'It's just hidden and disguised behind a Catholic, European exterior. I'm going to go and see what evidence I can find.'

'Spain a Moorish country?'

'Some Moors may have left,' I went on, 'but many stayed. They just became Christians and kept many of their Arabic customs – food, sayings, architecture, music. That kind of thing. Look at the faces – I'm always seeing people in the street who remind me of Arab or even Iranian friends.'

He started laughing.

'What's so funny?'

'Jasie, if this is a Moorish country, why don't they give me a job?' He slapped the glove box in front of him. 'Look at me! I'm a Moor. You think this is a

Moorish country? Why do they want to throw me out all the time, then? Yes, this is true. Spain, Al-Andalus, was once an Islamic country, a great Islamic country. But this is all history now.'

I couldn't deny he might be right and I was anxious not to allow too much romanticism to creep in. Nonetheless I had to keep my eyes open for what others had failed to see.

'The great age of tolerance and co-existence between Moors and Christians is over,' he said. 'In the past Muslims conquered the West. Now the West conquers the Muslims. Perhaps the Muslims will one day conquer Spain again. Then you can say Moorish Spain. But not now.'

Distracted by our conversation, I had failed to notice that the needle showing the engine temperature had swung over dramatically to the right. Steam began to appear from under the bonnet.

'We're overheating!'

It was an old car, and the school teacher who'd sold it to me had mumbled something about having to top up the water levels every week or so. But he'd seemed the over-cautious type, and I'd ignored his warning. I swerved the car towards the hard shoulder as quickly as I could, missing a camper van in the slow lane by only a few feet.

'It's all right, Jasie.'

A red warning light started glaring at me from the dashboard. We rolled into the narrow, gritty emergency lane and ground to a halt.

The bonnet burnt my hands as I lifted it up and the steam wrapped itself around my face.

'Radiator,' said Zine as he leant over beside me. He bent down almost double to have a look, supporting himself on my shoulder, then stood up and sniffed, turning away to go back inside. I was rather hoping he might know a thing or two about engines but it looked as if the two of us were as ignorant as each other. And we were stranded. Gazing up in the fuzzy light, no emergency phone was visible, and I resigned myself to trudging up the side of the motorway in the heat until I could find someone to help. A Gypsy had once stopped to help me in similar circumstances, silently and swiftly changing my tyre with his jack as though following an ancient travellers' code. But such instances were rare: you couldn't rely on it happening a second time. I looked down again at the engine. With any luck it wouldn't be too damaged, but I would be lucky to get back home that night. Might have to stay in a hotel. And what was I going to do with Zine?

At that moment he appeared once again by my side.

'I found some gum in the side pocket of the door,' he said, chewing away with his cheerful grin. The car's broken down, it's a searingly hot afternoon, lorries are growling past us only inches away and we're in the middle of nowhere. If we don't get knocked dead by an eighteen-wheel juggernaut we'll die of heat exhaustion. And he's looking for chewing gum?

He read the expression on my face and put his finger to his mouth to stop me from saying anything. Taking the white misshapen lump from between his teeth he bent double again over the engine and reached down with his hand.

'There,' he said, standing up. 'Got any water in the back?'

'What have you done?'

'I've plugged the hole in the radiator. It's stopped leaking. We just need to fill it up with more water and we're fine for another hundred kilometres.'

'Are you sure?' I thought he was pulling my leg.

'Jasie, trust me,' he laughed.

VALENCIA

'¡Hala!'
Two days after arriving safely in Valencia, we walked into the Plaza de la Virgen as a group of worshippers spilled out from the church after a late-night mass in honour of Valencia's patron – the Virgin of the Defenceless. Elderly women pushed past the Romanian beggars at the entrance, calling over to one another with expressions of joy and surprise as they past through the opening and closing leather-padded doors. I lost track of all the different religious feast days and celebrations through the course of the year, but tonight looked like a special occasion for devotees of the star-spangled statue of the mother of Jesus inside. La Cheperudeta, they called her – the hunch-back – for her oddly stooped posture.

'¡Hala!' The cries of the women could be heard all around the square.

We'd come out for dinner in the centre of town. It was a Friday, and the streets and squares of the Carmen, the old Arab quarter, were filled with people of all ages going out for a drink and meeting up with friends. Valencia had just been declared the noisiest city in Europe: much of the racket, I felt sure, came from the all-night restaurants and bars that lined many of the narrow lanes of the *casco histórico*. Valencianos prided themselves on being fiesta people, and not to have made the decibel top spot would probably have been a cause for shame. It was midnight already and we'd yet to sit down and eat anywhere – it was going to be a long night.

Zine had spent much of the previous day sleeping on the sofa bed in our sitting room, the cats sniffing curiously around the clothes he'd dropped on the floor and curling up around his legs. As ever moved to help someone in need, Salud had pulled out some old trousers and shirts of mine for him to wear: they fell loosely on him, but when they were tucked in and secured with a belt he just looked as if he'd been dieting a bit too hard. She was as concerned as I was that we should find him work as soon as possible, but the only real chance we had was with her father, an elderly orange farmer who lived south of the city. It was worth trying him out, but she was doubtful.

'He's getting old. I don't know if he takes people on any more.'

Nonetheless, we'd decided to head out with Zine to her parents' village the following day.

My voyage of discovery around Moorish Spain had just begun, and I was already back at home – all I'd managed to pick up was an out-of-work Moroccan. It wasn't the start I'd expected, and although I wanted to find Zine a job, and was genuinely concerned about him, I was wondering how long it would be before my journey got off the ground. Was it going to be a complete non-starter?

'¡*Hala!*' The cries from the church women came again.

'Listen,' said Zine, leaning over to me and pointing. 'What are they saying?'

'*Hala,*' I said. 'It's a common expression of surprise.'

It was a word I'd heard and used myself a thousand times, but for some reason, perhaps because I was talking to an Arab, as I repeated it to him that night in the square the penny dropped: it sounded remarkably like the Arabic *Allah. In sha' Allah* – Zine had come out with it in the car: 'God willing'. Muslims use it all the time when talking about the future, a constant reminder of the uncertainty of things. The phrase had been adopted into Spanish as *ojalá* as a way of expressing hope: friends of mine who had travelled into the Amazon jungle said you even found Indians using it.

Allah in Arabic was used in a whole host of sayings: *yallah*, meaning 'let's go'; *ma sha' Allah*, 'amazing'; or often just *Allah* on its own, much as we might say 'God'. If *in sha' Allah* had crossed over into Spanish, I couldn't see why *Allah* hadn't as well. You just changed the spelling: it sounded exactly the same.

I mentioned this to Zine.

'They're saying *Allah*?' he said, a dramatic expression of surprise on his face, his normally wide-open eyes stretching to almost abnormal proportions.

Salud was more interested in what looked like a street-theatre performance taking place on the other side of the square, great flaming torches lighting up a scene of colourfully painted faces and fantastical costumes.

'*Ole,*' I said, trying to catch her attention. 'That comes from Arabic, too, from *wallah* – "By God".'

She walked on.

'In Andalusian churches,' I explained to Zine, 'you often hear them shouting *ole* – the name of the God of Islam in a Christian church. But they don't even realize.'

I laughed. I had a fascination with such things – for me they were clues in my attempt to understand Spain's unique character: a culture which appeared to have been formed by two ostensibly opposed religions. I felt as if I'd unexpectedly stumbled on an important piece of evidence, one that had been staring me in the face for years. Yet Salud, as Spanish as ever, had yet to be infected by my enthusiasm for her country's Moorish past.

'So?' she said. '*Ole* is *ole*. They're not Muslims.'

As a flamenco dancer the word belonged to her, the emotive cry of *ole* being an essential part of any good performance. It didn't do for me to try to take it away from her.

'Yes, I know. But isn't it amazing . . .'

'They don't know they're saying *Allah*. It's just *ole*.'

Zine patted me on the back. 'I heard you,' he said.

I hung on to Salud as we climbed up the low step in the square. My leg still hurt from the farmer's blow, but the swelling wasn't as bad as I'd expected, and apart from a knotty tension in the muscle where he'd struck it seemed to be recovering well. A slight coloration of the skin was the only outward sign of what had happened. I was all right to walk, although it was painful, but I thought it best to keep it moving rather than resting for too long, so we'd brought Zine to see a little of the city.

Valencia, halfway up the east coast of Spain, is an often overlooked part of the country. Caught between Catalonia to the north and Madrid to the west, it is a sunny, Mediterranean place which, although it might try on occasion, never manages to thrust itself upon you in the way of so many Spanish regions.

'To understand Valencia you have to realize she's like a woman with her legs open,' Eduardo had once told me. 'She's there for you to discover.'

Since making it my home I'd often perceived a Moorishness to it, despite this being less obvious than in Andalusian cities. Christians had conquered Valencia in the thirteenth century around the same time as Córdoba and Seville, yet there was no Great Mosque or Arabian palace on display to prove the five hundred years it had spent as part of Al-Andalus; the legacy was more subtle.

The name Valencia itself came from the Romans: *terra valentia*. Yet almost all the towns and villages near by had Arabic-derived names: Alginet (*al-jannat* – the gardens), Alcácer (*al-qasr* – the castle), Alzira (*al-jazira* – the island). The countryside had remained home to thousands of Moors for centuries after Christians had taken over, farming the land and cultivating the famous oranges that the Arab conquerors had first brought to the area.

Then there were the people themselves. Valencians sometimes reminded me of Iranians, or perhaps the Lebanese – a link reinforced by the name Levante often given to this eastern coastal region. They were the merchants of Spain, the wheeler-dealers: wily, playful and slightly suspect. People from other parts of the country complained you could never trust a Valencian, that they were amiable at first, but it was impossible to develop a true friendship with them. *Mi casa es tu casa* – they would repeat the oft-heard Valencian phrase with a sarcastic sneer. But what

62

could be more Oriental than to offer your house to someone you've only just met? Arabs and Persians would often do the same.

Paella – Valencia's greatest contribution to Spanish cuisine and the nearest thing Spain has to a national dish – has a Middle Eastern connection in the rice and saffron that are its main ingredients: both were introduced by the Moors, the words *arroz* and *azafrán* coming from *ruzz* and *za'faran*. The name of the dish may come from the Arabic for leftovers – *al-baqiya* (the 'q' is often silent) – and it certainly echoes the Persian *polow* – a plate of rice stuffed with combinations of meat and vegetables, where the most sought-after bit, just as here, is the crusty layer of concentrated flavours near the bottom of the pan: the *socarraet*, as it is known in Valenciano.

And just as Valencians and Iranians both based their cuisine on rice dishes, so they shared a love of fire festivals. The biggest celebration in the Iranian year was Norouz – New Day, the ritual surrounding the spring equinox on 21 March. In Valencia it was Fallas on St Joseph's Day, which fell two days earlier. Enormous five-storey-high papier-mâché and wooden sculptures were built in every square and on every street corner, the city shut down for a week of parties, fire-cracker concerts and firework displays, and on the final day everything burnt to the ground in a bacchanalian orgy of flame. It felt like a combination of the siege of Stalingrad and the Last Night of the Proms.

The Persian equivalent was similar in many ways. During *chaharshambeh suri*, a couple of days before the equinox, men would jump over bonfires in the middle of the street. Valencians still jumped over their own bonfires at fiesta time, although this particular rite had been moved to the feast of St John the Baptist in July.

El Cid was another interesting example of the crossover of Moor and Christian in the city. Born in the northern Christian town of Medinaceli, Rodrigo Díaz, an undefeated general, had wandered round Spain fighting for both Muslim and Christian kings at different points in his career before finally taking over Valencia as a kind of personal fiefdom at the end of the eleventh century. Yet this was never a Christian 'Reconquest' – that lay almost a hundred and fifty years into the future. He ruled Christian subjects according to ancient Visigothic laws, and Muslims according to the law of the Qur'an. The title by which he was known was simply the Spanish pronunciation of the Arabic *al-sid* – an honorific meaning 'lord' or sometimes 'saint'. Moor or Christian? It wasn't easy to say. Although when the epic poem about his life, the *Poema de Mio Cid*, was composed some hundred years after his death, all mention of his having served Muslim rulers such as Al-Mu'tamin of Saragossa was systematically left out.

Valencia eventually fell to the Christians in 1238, yet the man who headed the campaign, Jaime I, 'the Conqueror', was also an interesting character. After negotiating a peace deal with the Muslim authorities in a tent pitched not more than fifty yards from where our flat now was, Jaime had divided the city up between the three different religions which were to share it – Christians in the middle, Muslims to the west and Jews to the east. The three areas are quite different in character even to this day. Little remains of the city he had known, but his mark is stamped all over in the form of a bat – his personal symbol and later the symbol of the city: everything from the football team emblem to street lamps have Jaime's bat somewhere on them. According to the legend an arrow shot at Jaime during the siege of Valencia hit a bat flying near by, thus saving the king's life. Others said the bat was a symbol of Jaime's initiation into a school of Islamic mysticism.

'How do you know about the origin of *ole*?' Zine asked me as we edged through the circle of crowds, moving towards the street-theatre show.

I told him that I had studied Arabic at Oxford, and was interested in flamenco.

'Have you been to Arab countries?'

'I lived for a while in Alexandria as a student,' I said.

'Hmpf. Egyptians,' he sniffed. I recognized in him a knee-jerk dislike of the culturally powerful 'eastern' Arab country. Moroccans saw themselves firmly as *maghrebis* – westerner Arabs – and sometimes resented the prevalence of Egyptian films and TV programmes.

Salud grabbed my arm and pulled me towards the performance. 'Look! It's Lucía.'

I saw a young woman crouched low and screaming, her hair tied up in twisting orange and blue rubber tubes, eyes painted thick black and with a thin blue piece of semi-transparent material wrapped around her body, her pierced tongue sticking out. Lucía was a young friend of Salud who'd spent years working in street-theatre companies, often travelling to perform across Spain and in Portugal and France. She was there in the show now, playing some kind of sci-fi witch, it seemed. Not that she'd been typecast, I thought: she was one of the jolliest and most open people I knew in the city.

There is a peculiar Spanish passion for street theatre, one I'd never been able to share, although the dream-like costumes and brightly painted faces could be fun to watch. Sometimes they told stories, and there were groups that worked principally with children. But often there didn't appear to be any discernible thread to events, the actors simply representing ideas or concepts with their costumes and movements.

'In Marrakesh they have something like this,' Zine said, leaning his head in to look over my shoulder.

I turned to listen to him above the noise of the performance.

'In the main square, the Jma el Fna,' he explained. 'Storytellers get up and enact old folk tales, sometimes in groups.'

Surprised, I prodded him to tell me more. My comments on the word *hala* had perhaps given him an idea of what I was looking for.

'They call them *halqas*,' he went on. 'It means "circle". People group in a circle to hear the story-teller. Like we're doing now. They do it all over Morocco, but it's famous in Marrakesh. That's like the university for storytellers. They have snake-charmers and all kinds of people as well.'

I looked back at Lucia's show with renewed interest: she was doing cartwheels while a girl dressed as a cat sang the Valencian regional anthem. Hard to imagine there could be a Moorish link here, but you never knew. Perhaps, I thought, revising my earlier ideas, finding Zine wasn't going to hamper things after all: it might even turn out to be a stroke of luck.

Half an hour later, having changed in the toilets of a

nearby bar, Lucía joined us to go and find a place to eat.

'This is Zine,' I said, introducing them.

'I saw you in the audience,' she said, kissing him on the cheeks.

We went to a sandwich bar in the heart of the Carmen. The streets were packed with people, all squeezing in between stray cars as they got lost in the labyrinth of alleyways. Black Africans stood at the side selling bootleg CDs and wooden sculptures of giraffes, while a woman with white hair and a wall-eye sat at a fold-up table offering to read tarot cards. One o'clock in the morning and it felt like the busiest hour of the day.

Lucía knew the owner of the bar and insisted on ordering for Zine, smiling broadly at him as we made a toast to his finding work.

'Oh my God!' she screamed as the waiter walked away with our order. 'It's got pork in it!'

Zine burst out laughing. 'I don't mind. Really. I can drink wine too. Look.' And he took another sip from his glass.

'*Ay, perdón*,' she said. 'I just thought . . . Never mind.'

'My parents didn't drink alcohol,' he said, 'but now it's common in Morocco. Why not?'

'*Didn't?*' Lucía asked. I too had noticed his use of the past tense, but felt it rude to ask more.

'They're both dead,' he said. 'My father when I was a child, my mother when I was thirteen.'

'So you're an orphan,' Lucía blurted out. 'I mean . . . that's right, isn't it?'

'Yes. I lived with my uncle and cousins in Casablanca.'

67

He seemed happy to tell this very personal story to the virtual strangers we were, and showed no sign of even considering that he might have had a tough childhood. He was proud, though, and something about his tone of voice gave me the impression that there was more to it – some difficulty with his uncle, perhaps.

'You speak Spanish really well,' Lucía said.

'I learnt in Tangier,' he said. 'You can see Spain from Tangier: of course I had to learn the language.'

Lucía laughed with him and held out her blue and white packet of L&M cigarettes. He reached out and took one off her, leaning forwards as she flicked her lighter for him. Salud glanced at me with a raised eyebrow from across the table.

We ate and talked. Salud and Lucía gossiped about actors they both knew from when they'd worked together, while Zine and I half listened in, watching the parade of night people passing to and fro in the street in front of us. A man dressed in a nappy and white boots was jumping up and down, dancing outside the door of the disco opposite.

'How long have you been in Spain?'

After a brief lull, Lucía started asking Zine more questions. I was surprised that he didn't mind this, but he talked at length about the years he'd spent in Tangier before coming over, hanging out with other young men looking for a chance to get across the Strait.

'I was lucky: I lived with my aunt. Many of them slept outdoors. We'd do bits of work whenever we could find it, saving the money to cross over to Spain. It's expensive. My aunt used to complain, though. Said I should stay in Morocco. She thought I'd end up as a rent boy over here, or something.'

'How did you get across?' Lucía asked. Her smile had been replaced by an expression of deep concern.

'Boat,' Zine said. 'They had to push me in because I was scared of the water. Just a little wooden boat with an engine at the back. But I'd been waiting for my chance for years. The farmers organized it. We crossed at night: you have to avoid all the patrols. Few of us had blankets; we were allowed just one bag each.

'It smelt like rotten fish,' he added with a laugh. 'I was almost sick.'

'And you got over all right?'

'Yes, of course. Then they took us straight to the farm where Jasie found me.' And he patted me on the shoulder.

Lucía's steady gaze barely wavered.

'You poor thing,' she said when he had finished telling her about the mafia set-up and our fight to escape. '*No hay mal que dure cien años*, they say – Bad things never last a hundred years.'

He smiled at her and she giggled. I could tell from Lucía's eyes that Salud and I were fading from view.

It seemed inevitable that we would return without Zine to the flat later that night. It was almost six in the morning – in a few hours we were due to take him to Salud's parents' house.

'We're going home,' I said. 'You guys staying on?'

They'd spent the last hour kissing at every opportunity; Salud and I had deliberately gone together to order drinks at the various bars we went to over the course of the night to allow them moments on their own. For couples to show affection in public was common in Spain, but even we were surprised at the sudden bond that had developed between them.

'We'll come round to pick you up,' Salud said as he and Lucía walked off in the direction of her flat, bodies pressed close to one another.

'Lucía,' I said as we turned the corner. 'She doesn't hang about.'

'I think they'll make a lovely couple,' said Salud.

ALZIRA

Vicenta moved around the dark kitchen with a heaviness, burdened by the weight of her ageing body, but also by something else. Sadness, perhaps, at having denied something of herself almost her entire life.

She breathed sharply and shallowly through her nose, opening her mouth once in a while as though gasping for air. Her heart was frail, yet it sometimes seemed you could almost hear its faint little tickety-tick beating underneath the layers of heavy clothes.

'My husband doesn't like this, but I'm making it because you're here,' she said, rubbing sweet smoked paprika with her thick fingers into roasted almonds she had just pulled from the oven. 'You need very fine salt, otherwise the crystals stick in one place.'

It was one of my favourites – a simple local dish. One of just half a dozen or more she was preparing for lunch that afternoon: fried anchovies, stuffed peppers, roast aubergines with garlic and olive oil, and sheep's milk cheese laced with quince jam.

Sitting on a stool in a corner as she worked – she would never let me help – I drew the sweat off my temples, hoping that a breeze might make it through the tiny window and cool us down.

'*¡Abuela!*' One of the children ran into the kitchen. 'When will lunch be ready?'

'Soon. Here, take this through carefully to your grandfather.' And she handed the boy a glass of beer to carry down the corridor. Maybe this would soften the old man up before I presented him with a Moroccan looking for work. 'I'm not a racist,' he had often declared over Sunday lunches. 'We are all *personas*.' Yet bringing him face to face with a *moro* would put his statement to the test. Salud had often been ticked off as a child when she took him at face value and in the spirit of brotherly love had brought Gypsy friends home from school. Now she was with Zine at the bar round the corner, waiting for my signal to come round with our surprise guest.

There was a crackling, spitting sound as Salud's mother placed the flour-dipped anchovies into the hot fat, a seafood smell spreading through the kitchen.

For a brief moment I was back in my flat in Alexandria. That smell was so familiar. Every Friday, without fail, my Coptic neighbour, Iskandar the chemist, who lived in the flat downstairs, would start cooking fish at dawn, the scent lifting up through my bedroom window as Khalid, my landlord, and his enormous family arrived promptly at half past seven to pick me up for a day on his private beach.

'*Yallah, ya Jasie,*' his delightful seven-year-old son would shout up to my window from the street. Why all Arabs had a problem pronouncing my name I had never worked out.

'Let's go!' I could quite happily sleep through the dawn call to prayer, but something about that kid's

73

voice went straight to the wake-up nerve in my brain, no matter what efforts I'd gone to the night before to anaesthetize it. Almost breaking my ankles as I tripped up in the corridor putting my trousers on at top speed, I would appear in the doorway one minute and thirty seconds later, barely conscious and stinking of fish and booze on the holiest day in the Islamic week, having to squeeze onto the back seat of their tiny car with a child on each knee. Great for my Arabic, I kept telling myself. Kids are fantastic for learning foreign languages, even if you do want to throttle them to death. But Khalid was the chief of the local prison. If he invited me to his private beach, I had to go. You didn't argue with a guy who pushed people out of windows for a living.

Here in Vicenta's kitchen, the food could easily sit alongside dishes from North Africa or the Middle East. She had never read cookbooks: her recipes and techniques had been passed down orally from mother to daughter over centuries. As I watched her prepare meatballs in tomato sauce, the links seemed all the more evident: their Spanish name, *albóndigas*, was a memory of the original Arabic word, *al-banadiq*; the pan she was cooking them in, a *cazuela*, came from the word *qas'a*, meaning 'bowl'. Four, perhaps five hundred years previously, an Arabic voice was speaking; a neighbour passing on a recipe to her Christian friend using the mixed Spanish-Arabic patois of the time. Or, during the Inquisition, a Morisco mother was speaking a half-forgotten language to her Christianized daughter, who could understand, but not speak, this strange and illegal tongue of her ancestors' fast-disappearing culture.

Salud's father was smoking his pipe in the living

room when I walked in, trying amid the chaos of playing, screaming children to concentrate on a TV documentary about the mating habits of Amazonian tapirs. His neat round head seemed too small for the broad shoulders on which it sat, and his gigantic arms, moulded by decades of hard physical work in the fields, looked as if they belonged to a different body altogether – the closest match they could find at the time in the local arm-transplant hospital. The ability of the man to instil fear in his own children – Salud sometimes told me of the beatings he'd given her and her sister – had waned with age, and now his growlings at his grandchildren as they fell over him in their hide-and-seek games went mostly unheard.

'Stop throwing those beer mats.' An aunt or uncle was more likely to be imposing discipline these days. Still, he went to his fruit fields every day, despite being in semi-retirement. And if his mood looked as if it was swinging to dangerous levels of grumpiness, you could always get him talking about the finer points of orange harvesting. When I had dared to suggest that oranges and most citrus fruits had in fact been introduced to Spain by the Moors, the familiar slightly dazed look that most Spaniards assume when presented with this kind of stuff came over his face. In many ways, though, his whole livelihood depended on the Moorish legacy: the Romans had laid foundations for the great market garden that circled Valencia, but the Arabs had brought the necessary irrigation know-how to convert it into one of the most fertile plains in Europe. Clues lay in the vocabulary farmers used: an irrigation channel was known as an *acequia* (or *séquia* in Valenciano – the local language), which came from the Arabic *al-saqiya*. The fruits and vegetables themselves had Middle Eastern names: orange – *naranja* in Spanish – came from the Persian *naranj*; artichokes, or *alcachofas*, came from the Arabic *al-kharshuf*; spinach, or *espinacas*, from *isbinaj*; aubergine, or *berenjena*, from *bidinjan*. The list was long. The running of the irrigation system was still overseen today by a local court set up during the reign of Abd al-Rahman II in the ninth century. During the Moorish period it had met inside the mosque itself, but now the Tribunal de las Aguas held its sessions outside the Gothic cathedral, standing on the site of the former Islamic temple. Its Moorish origins were still evident from the time the court sat – every Thursday at midday, the traditional day for meetings in an Islamic context, Thursday being the last day of the working week. The bailiff of the court was known as *el alguacil*, a title derived from the Arabic *al-wazir*, or minister.

'Young people today don't know the meaning of hard work.' Salud's father turned away from the television as his programme finished. Looking at the size of his forearms I wasn't about to argue with him. He was a constant reminder of our soft-living age.

'This year's been terrible – all over Europe. Never known a year like it. Rains everywhere. I know 'cause I've seen it on the telly. It's a window on the world, that thing.'

'Bad crop?'

'There was a freak hail storm the other day – damaged everything. It's only good for juice now.'

This had the potential to throw out our plans, the hope being that as we moved into the harvest period he would appreciate an extra pair of hands in his orchards. But with things not looking good the chances of getting Zine a job seemed to be diminishing. I decided to broach the subject straight away.

'All right,' he said when I told him my friend was waiting in a bar with Salud. 'Is he English?' I shook my head. 'Oh, well. Show him in. As long as he's not Moroccan. They never lift a finger.'

Two and a half hours later we were back in the car, bellies full but no work for Zine. My efforts to pretend he was Algerian hadn't really paid off and Salud's father had simply sat back in front of the TV after lunch and ignored him. But then I wasn't sure if it was a general dislike of *moros* on his part or simply that he didn't have enough work to offer. In the past, when the Moriscos were still working on the land after the Reconquest, the Christian landowner's saying was *Quien tiene moro tiene oro* – something like 'Moors are worth their weight in gold'. The new Christian arrivals from the north had relied on them for their agricultural nous, at least until their final expulsion. Nowadays the stereotype was of North Africans being lazy and untrustworthy.

'He's hardly got any orchards left now – he's sold most of them off,' Salud said as we left. 'I don't think he can afford to pay anyone to work for him.'

I was sure she was right, but we were still facing the problem of what to do with Zine. I couldn't leave Valencia to continue with my trip until we'd got him settled in some way.

'You can drop me off at Lucía's place,' Zine said as we reached the city centre, leaning between us from the back seat like a cockerel, head jerking excitedly in small sideways movements. 'She's dining Moroccan tonight. Ha, ha.'

Still, he'd landed on his feet in one sense.

MORISCOS

*I*t was Michaelmas the day we left – the clearest day of the year – driving south on the old Játiva road towards Alicante. The rains of the previous week had cleaned the air and the mountains that ringed the city on three sides like a crescent moon rippled a welcoming purple-green, sharp edges against the blue-white sky. The area was at its best like this, and the unrestricted light bathed the blighting megastores and warehouses that cut deep into the orange orchards with a softening haze. It augured well, I thought. Recommencing my journey on such a day could only be a good thing.

Zine sat beside me smoking a packet of L&M cigarettes and reading about Iraq in the newspaper. Lucía had failed to show up that morning to see us off; from his silence it seemed the separation had been more difficult than he'd expected. But he still needed work, and despite trying everything we could – even asking around the Arab bars – we'd been unable to find him anything in Valencia. The problem was, as always, his lack of paperwork.

* * *

'There's always Tío Sergio,' Salud had said. 'He has Moroccans working for him.'

Like his elder brother, Salud's uncle was also a farmer, but had moved away from Valencia twenty years before down to the village of Niebla in Andalusia, near the south-western border with Portugal. It was one of the centres of agricultural work for North Africans, great fruit fields the size of cities filling the gaps between the few, underpopulated villages in the area. After hesitating for a day, we gave Uncle Sergio a ring. Cash in hand, of course. No, he didn't have any paperwork.

From the expression on Salud's face as she spoke to him, I could tell he was reluctant to agree. You didn't give a job to someone you'd never met before just based on a phone call, especially someone who could land you in jail. But the fact was he did need people, and Salud was his favourite niece.

'*Tráelo y veremos*,' he said. 'Bring him and we'll see. *No prometo na.*'

And so now, three weeks since he'd saved me from the mafia farmers, Zine was back in the passenger seat of my car once more, homeless, jobless and 'illegal', but a useful person to have around if the car played up again. I had planned to travel through Andalusia and the south in my search for Musa's treasure anyway, I reminded myself. Besides, putting him on a train or a bus would have been risky, as he was more likely to be picked up by the police that way in an ID check. Yet we still had to be careful: Spanish friends of mine had been asked for their papers just because they had darkish skin and wore old clothes. It was clearly safer for him to come with me.

There was a complication, though: Uncle Sergio

could only take him on in another fortnight's time, but I needed to set off now: two of the people I wanted to meet along my way would be unavailable if I left it any longer. Which meant the two of us stuck together travelling for some time.

At first I'd felt a reluctance about bringing him along: travelling alone meant greater flexibility, not having to worry about someone else's moods. And this was a very personal trip, too, in many ways – a journey to discover more of Spain and to see, perhaps once and for all, if it really was a country I could feel at home in. But reluctance melted into a feeling of inevitability.

'At least you'll have a Moor with you in your search for Moorish Spain,' Salud said.

Zine had already given me a couple of insights into Spanish life that I might otherwise have missed. I was just worried about the authorities getting hold of him before I'd made good my promise.

Something of his character had become apparent in his relationship with Lucía. I had never known her so happy as in that brief time they were together. Although she had had a string of boyfriends, something about Zine seemed to rub off on her, producing a fullness of being and sense of peace that all her friends had remarked on. The occasional voice might have warned her against a relationship with a *moro*, but in the eyes of anyone who knew her well the arrival of Zine had been a life-affirming experience for her.

'*Gracias*,' she'd whispered to me one night as we stepped out of a bar together just a fraction before Salud and Zine behind us. And she'd held my hand tightly – no need to explain anything.

The effect of the relationship on Zine was harder to

tell, as I'd barely known him before the two of them had hooked up. I'd been amazed at the speed with which it had happened, but it was obvious they had bonded quite powerfully. My original impressions of him were confirmed and reinforced, if anything, by the joy I saw in Lucía; he was upbeat, dynamic and clearly ready to jump at opportunities, although I never had the impression at any stage that he was simply cruising for a meal ticket. He'd rarely been at the flat with us after the first week and had handed me back my old clothes when Lucía had bought him some new ones. I'd told him not to bother, but he insisted.

We met up every day as we tried over and again to find him work – driving to other farms, calling friends, checking the small ads in *Levante* over glasses of cold *horchata*. I had been the one to start losing heart, yet he had never for a moment doubted we would succeed.

'I trust you, Jasie. Really. Everything will be fine, I know.'

Whether it was being in love or just his nature, I couldn't tell. If anything, though, it was, perversely, this unyielding positive attitude in him that made me have doubts: I had yet to see a darker side to him, and when it came it would catch me unawares.

The obvious way to start was by heading south. I felt certain that Moorish culture had seeped into all Spain in some form or other, but in the south and Andalusia – the region whose name derived from Al-Andalus – the influence was more immediate. This was home to the Alhambra and the Great Mosque at Córdoba – the two greatest architectural legacies of Spanish Islam. Skin tone was generally darker, hair blacker, and complicated geometrical Islamic design work could be found on everything from bathroom tiles to stickers on car bumpers. Once I'd soaked up as much as I could in Andalusia and honed my senses, I planned to continue around the peninsula by passing into Portugal, returning to Spain through the central plains of Castille before heading for Catalonia: I already had leads that suggested this far north-eastern corner might prove fruitful in my search.

Orchards of short bushy green trees peppered with bright oranges rushed past on either side of the road. To the east sat the town of Manises, today the home of Valencia airport, but still the capital of the region's ceramic industry, as it had been since the Arabs introduced complex lustre techniques a thousand years before. The popes and kings of Europe had once been proud to own plates and jugs crafted by the Moors of Valencia, with their typical decoration patterns based on wild bryony.

'They lack our faith,' Cardinal Ximénez de Cisneros once said of the Moorish craftsmen, 'but we lack their works.'

'All these villages,' I said to my silent passenger, trying to start conversation, 'used to be inhabited by your ancestors. Look, there: Aldaia. From *al-day'a* in Arabic – village or farm.'

He said nothing, just drawing on his cigarette and nodding to show he was listening.

'Moors stayed on in many areas for hundreds of years after the Reconquest,' I said. 'Especially in the countryside.'

The Kingdom of Granada – and with it Al-Andalus as a whole – had come to an end in the late fifteenth century. The Spanish kingdoms of Castille and Aragon were united by the marriage of King Ferdinand and

Queen Isabel, and a final attack was launched on the Moorish south. After a ten-year fight, the city of Granada finally fell on 2 January 1492. In August of the same year all Jews were expelled from Spain. Two months later Columbus touched land on the other side of the Atlantic. Many Muslims stayed on in Spain rather than emigrate, living for the most part in agricultural areas such as the Alpujarras valley south of Granada, or in Valencia and Aragón. Persecuted by the Inquisition, in 1521 the Moriscos, 'little Moors' as they were then called, were forced to convert en masse to Christianity and banned from reading or writing Arabic.

The irony was not lost on me of our trying to find farm work for Zine now, when for their final years in Spain the Moriscos had been permitted to do little else. Not much had really changed in four centuries.

'What happened?' Zine asked, looking out of the window. It was the first thing he'd said all day.

'Many remained Muslim in secret,' I said. 'But there was a rebellion. Moors living near Granada rose up in 1568. Sparked off the most savage European war that century.'

Eventually, some forty years later in 1609, the king decided to kick them all out – perhaps 300,000 or perhaps three million. No one was really sure. Almost nine hundred years after the first Muslims crossed the Strait of Gibraltar, Spain once more became 'pure'.

'They were actually thinking of castrating them until that point to keep their numbers down,' I said.

'Like animals.'

The two religious communities had become polarized in the years just before the expulsion: in Valencia in the late 1500s condemned Moors were given the choice of being executed as Muslims or Christians. If they chose the former they were taken down to the river and stoned to death. If they chose to convert, they would be hanged in the usual way in the market square. Opting for the quicker way to die, many Muslims went through the motions of turning Catholic, only to renounce the faith of their executors just as the noose was being placed around their neck. Christian onlookers grew wise to this, though, and as the condemned man publicly declared himself a Muslim with cries of 'Allah' and 'Muhammad', they unleashed a hail of stones and rocks at him. Many spectators were hurt or even killed in the mêlée. By the next morning, however, not a trace of the riot would be left, as Moriscos would have come overnight and picked up every stone to take them away for safe-keeping – sacred relics of their brother's 'martyrdom'.

'Not everyone thought the expulsion of the Moriscos was a good idea, though,' I continued. I decided, given Zine's low mood, that it might be better to keep the execution story to myself. 'Cardinal Richelieu described it as "the most barbarous act in human annals".'

'Richelieu? He was French.'

'There were Spaniards against it as well. Just a few years beforehand some Valencian aristocrat even built a secret mosque for Muslims working for him, saying they should pretend to be Christians but remain Muslim on the inside. They had to pretend not to speak Arabic, and some were even arrested just for eating couscous.'

'Try eating *my* couscous: it'll put you in hospital,' he said. 'Seriously,' he went on as I laughed, 'I'm the worst cook I know. Even Lucía said so.'

He fell silent again at the mention of her name, stubbing his cigarette out in the ashtray below the radio and immediately taking another out to light.

I wanted to ask him how they'd left it. It was becoming obvious they'd had an argument, but it was unclear if they'd finished for good or were planning on seeing each other again. Was he just annoyed, or was I with someone suffering from a broken heart? I decided to wait. He might tell me himself anyway.

We drove up into the coastal mountains as our journey continued south. Játiva, home of the first paper mill in Europe, came into view on the other side of the sun-filled valley. It was a small town, concentrated around the base of a rocky hill surrounded by pine woods and more fruit trees. Paper-making had reached here in the tenth century after the Arabs learned it from Chinese artisans on capturing Samarkand in Afghanistan, and most of the first paper to reach Christian hands had been exported from this very town. Cheaper and easier to produce than papyrus and vellum, paper, which was then made from straw and rice, was exported to Christian territories from the twelfth century, although it took a while to catch on. What had made it popular, though, was the invention of printing techniques: 'When in the fifteenth century book production was commercialized by the introduction of mechanical apparatus, paper became an essential material in the production of machine-made books,' one historian, A. H. Christie, had written. Without paper, brought by the Moors to Europe, the printing press would never have got off the ground.

Strangely, printing took much longer to establish itself in the Islamic world, where the work of the scribe was faithfully preserved for much longer. Yet it was thanks to this innovation that books and learning were eventually able to spread to a greater audience in the West.

Játiva was a picturesque yet forgotten place, now. A church, a cluster of old houses, a discotheque in an abandoned olive-oil press. Nothing showed where the paper factory had once stood. The ruins of an old Arab citadel watched over the lush valley, the only reminder of the key role the town had once played.

The great Moorish poet Ibn Khafaja, born in the neighbouring town of Alzira, had often idolized this garden landscape:

The stars shone there like live embers,
The night's breath perfumed with ambergris:
Fragrant orange blossom mingled with rose
Like a sweet white mouth smiling as it kisses a
    cheek.

We drove on, into the mountain range that lay before us like a wall: a narrow melting road threading over the peaks our passage to the south.

WINDMILLS

'*Bismillah al-rahman al-rahim.*'

Pedro grinned as he opened the gate for us to enter. 'Good to see you again, *mi querido Watson.*'

He used his usual name for me, confusing my surname with that of Sherlock Holmes's sidekick. The house looked unchanged: the same whitewashed walls, green shutters and jasmine-scented garden where we had sat in wrought-iron chairs when I'd first arrived in Spain ten years before. I had fond memories of this house – Pedro had taken me under his wing back then and I had him to thank not only for my connection with the country, but in many ways for the journey I was making now: he had been the first to plant the idea in my mind as one Arabist to another that Moorishness ran deep in Spain, and he seemed to be engaged in a personal campaign to hold on to as much of it as possible before it disappeared. 'In the name of Allah, the Compassionate, the Merciful,' he would mutter whenever we sat down to eat. A Spanish Arabist and a church-going professor of Islamic philosophy, he was as happy reading the Qur'an as the Bible, and had never been easy to pigeon-hole.

From the family-run restaurant near by came the warm lingering smell of earlier lunches: fried garlic, prawns, artichokes, and the most characteristic Spanish cooking smell of all, grilled red peppers – a sweet, smoky reminder of the Moors who had first made them popular. Behind the house the pomegranate trees were in bloom, their deep-orange flowers burning among the dark-green leaves, while at the front palms towered high above the flat terrace roof. Pedro and I had often spent evenings watching the stars up there: the *azotea*. It had been the first Spanish word I'd learnt the Arabic etymology for: *al-suth*, 'roof'.

Yet the surroundings had changed since I had last visited. It had been a quiet, under-developed area reached along dirt roads with empty, stony fields stretching for miles on all sides. Dotted here and there were isolated, understated villas, tall pine trees, or the occasional goatherd with his animals, and there was a fine view of the sea. But now there were rows upon rows of tower blocks and 'chalets' with underground car parks and communal swimming pools. The little track in front of Pedro's house had yet to be tarmacked, but everywhere there were razor-sharp white lines, STOP signs, paved sidewalks and black ribbons of roads to provide easy access for the commuters who had turned this into another suburb of the ever-sprawling city on the coast. The patch of land between Pedro's house and his sister's, like so many others in Albufereta (Arabic: *al-buhaira* – the little sea), where our little white cat used to hunt sparrows in the mornings, had been filled in with a brown, concrete condominium. Cars were parked in a tight row along one edge of the road, while a sign had already been put up in the field opposite giving notice of the building project soon to start work there – more houses, with more underground car parks and communal swimming pools. We had always expected this to happen, if not actually said so. And now it had. Pedro's house stood in the middle of it all, an ark preserving something of other times.

'You've brought your Moroccan friend,' Pedro smiled as we stepped inside. '*Ahlan wa sahlan*,' he said to Zine. 'Welcome. I've just made some tea.' The pencil moustache above his top lip, a touch greyer these days, quivered as he spoke.

'*Hola*,' I said, kissing him on the cheeks.

'*Allah*,' he said, shaking Zine's hand. 'Have you realized every day millions of Spaniards and South Americans greet each other like Muslims?'

'Is that where *hola* comes from?' I asked.

'I thought you already knew.'

We skirted around the rosemary bushes to the jasmine enclave at the heart of his garden, and sat down at the table already laid out with a pewter teapot and china cups and saucers. Afternoon tea was one of the major rituals in the Pedro household – something he'd picked up from living in London years before. But he always made sure there was a Moorish flavour to it: a tangled bunch of fresh mint from the garden placed inside the pot, and a hookah lit and ready to smoke by the side of his chair.

'Allah. Hola,' I said to myself. Like *ole* or *hala*, *hola* sounded as though it came from the same word. The common way of pronouncing 'Allah' in Arabic was to stress the 'l' sound in such a way that the initial 'a' sounded more like an 'o' or a 'u', as in 'ulla'. The words sounded very similar.

'It's true,' said Zine. 'They're the same. I hear people in the street saying Allah all the time. Allah! Allah!' he called out, pretending to wave at imaginary passers-by.

'The Arabs ruled here for eight hundred years,' Pedro butted in. 'Some of us still haven't left.'

He drew long and deeply on the hookah sitting on the floor by his chair, a hot, bubbling sound filling the gap in the conversation for a second before he blew out a long slow stream of smoke through his mouth and nose, scattering the mosquitoes that had gathered around the bare lightbulb hanging above his head.

'Do you remember Kenneth Clark?' he went on. 'Wrote a book called *Civilisation*.' He explained that when the documentary version was shown on Spanish television it had to be pulled halfway through, as Clark announced that Spain had done 'little or nothing to enlarge the human mind'.

'This is the country that introduced Aristotle and higher mathematics to Europe, and yet this man could say that in full confidence,' Pedro said. This was a common trap to fall into: of seeing only *Christian* Spain. He laughed.

'Averroes, Maimonides and Ibn al-Arabi were all Spanish, Watson. Three of the greatest thinkers of the Middle Ages. Until as recently as only twenty years ago it was as though they never existed. Or only belonged to *them* – the Arabs. Yet the influence of these wise men can still be felt today.'

Without any prompting, Pedro had slipped effortlessly into his theme; it was as though he could read my mind. This was exactly what I hoped to find out more about.

'So how is this influence still felt today?' I asked.

'Europe – and Spain,' he explained, 'see themselves

93

as the product of Judeo-Christian culture built on Classical foundations.' It was a familiar image, one that had been reinforced by the Renaissance and which perhaps only today had begun to weaken – the Greek and Latin worlds had essentially combined with Christian beliefs and the result was what we termed the West. There was a gaping hole in this picture, though.

'The debt to the Islamic world is greater than most people are aware.'

'Of course,' said Zine.

'Europe was lifted out of the Dark Ages precisely because Muslims, Christians and Jews integrated in Spain,' Pedro carried on. These three religions had been at each other's throats since before the Crusades. You just had to look at the situation today, with the Israeli–Palestinian conflict, war against Al-Qa'ida and US troops swarming down on the Gulf. Things hadn't changed, it seemed.

'Yet a great moment in human history took place right here in Spain when they got together.' It had begun in the late eleventh century. Christian forces in the north of the peninsula took advantage of internal divisions within the Moorish state and launched a major push south, securing their first important victory with the conquest of Toledo, the former Visigothic capital, in 1085. This was in the years just before the first Crusade, and was the first significant episode in the Reconquest. Yet it also sparked off one of the most important periods of interchange between Christians, Muslims and Jews: after falling into Christian hands, Toledo became a major centre of translation into Latin of Arabic learning, and for the first time Europeans had access to works by Muslim mathematicians such as Al-Khwarizmi and polymaths such as Ibn Sina (Avicenna, as he was called in Europe, known for his writings on medicine and music). For the first time they could also read Aristotle and Plato, whose books finally made it into the European lingua franca, having been translated two hundred years earlier from Greek into Arabic. This learning laid the groundwork for the later 'rebirth' of Europe.

Having studied Islamic history, I knew something of what Pedro was saying. But few people at university had ever stressed its importance as he did. The Moors were often regarded as a detail in Spanish history – 'important but not fundamental'. The Inquisition – the precursor to many of the acts of mass terror, racism and ethnic cleansing that marked the twentieth century – had done its best to wipe out the Jewishness and Moorishness of Spain: a continuation of the Reconquest on the home front once the military battles had been won. 'Hearts and minds, they would call it today,' Pedro said. Four hundred years after the Toledo experiment with intellectual diversity, a religiously unified society was deemed necessary for the new imperial state. Spain was expanding into America, it was the richest and most powerful country in Europe in the sixteenth century, yet it felt insecure: threatened both by Muslim Turks and by religious reformist movements in Europe. Spanish society itself, with its large Moorish and Jewish minorities and long tradition of liberal thought, could well prove to be the state's worst enemy – a myriad of fifth columns waiting to be activated from the outside. Paranoia set in: all religious difference must be eradicated, free thinking snuffed out. And the instrument for doing this was the

Inquisition, with its bonfires, instruments of torture and spreading of fear. Spain has been in denial ever since.

'The Inquisition wasn't completely successful, however,' Pedro said. 'It changed Spain's image of itself, and perhaps the image it gives to the rest of the world, yet nine hundred years of Moorish presence on the peninsula cannot be wiped away by a few autos-da-fé. Certain things slipped under their noses, precisely because they were disguised, invisible to the persecutors, even heralded as "Christian". How better to escape your tormentors than to claim you are even more orthodox than they?'

He smiled at this remark. Wasn't that what the legend of Musa's treasure was all about?

Zine pulled on the denim jacket Lucía had given him, which had been hanging on the back of the chair. Just a few weeks into autumn and the evenings were beginning to feel chilly.

'Do you want to go inside?' Pedro asked.

Zine shook his head and pulled out a cigarette from the packet lying half-open on the table.

'Here's what I mean,' Pedro continued after a pause to pour more hot tea. He handed out shortbread biscuits from a tin with a red tartan pattern on the lid. 'I went to mass at the church near the French Lycée last week. Hardly anyone there. The priest was reading from the gospel and commentating on it, the usual thing. But it struck me that what he was saying about love could have come from the mouth of Ibn al-Arabi himself.'

An Islamic mystic and writer known to the West as 'Doctor Maximus', and one of the greatest Spaniards who ever lived, according to some, Ibn al-Arabi had been born in the nearby city of Murcia in the twelfth century. His work, along with Arabic legends about Muhammad's journey to heaven, directly influenced Dante in the writing of his *Divine Comedy* – the 'greatest single instance of Muslim influence on Western literature', one scholar has said. Of all the Sufis in Al-Andalus, he had become the most celebrated, and groups had sprung up all over the world dedicated to studying his life and writings.

'"Love is the faith I hold: wherever turn / His camels, still the one true faith is mine," ' Pedro recited. 'Who does that sound like, if not Jesus? Ibn al-Arabi, Jesus, it's all the same thing. This is why Spain is still a Moorish country. Your friend here already knows all this.' And he nodded towards Zine.

I wasn't quite sure how Zine would take Pedro. The problem was you were never sure which Pedro might make an appearance. Sometimes, if he felt the company wasn't right, he could slip inside his shell and sit quietly, barely making the effort to engage even in ordinary chit-chat. Yet now here he was in all his heterodox splendour, pouring tea for a North African he'd never met before, effectively saying that Islam and Christianity were the same thing.

'Christian and Muslim mystics spoke the same language here,' Pedro said. 'Listen to this.' And he began reciting again:

> *'No me mueve, mi Dios, para quererte*
> *el cielo que me tienes prometido*
> *ni me mueve el infierno tan temido*
> *para dejar por eso de ofenderte.'*

'Tis not the promised heavens
That cause me to love you, O God,
Nor fear of hell
That prevents me from offending you.

'OK? Now listen to *this*: "Oh Lord! If I worship you from fear of hell, cast me into hell, and if I worship you from desire of paradise, deny me paradise." '

The poem, he explained, was anonymous, but believed to be by the great Spanish mystic St John of the Cross, writing in the sixteenth century. The second statement was uttered by the female saint Rabia al-Adawiya in Iraq, eight hundred years earlier.

'One is a Christian, the other Muslim, yet they say the same thing.'

'Of course,' Zine repeated. I looked at him from the corner of my eye. Much of this appeared to be familiar to him. Arabs I'd known had often been very proud of the influence of their culture on the West, but still, I suspected this was fairly specialist information Pedro was passing on.

'The crossovers are everywhere,' Pedro continued, crumbs falling onto his pale-blue shirt from the biscuit he was trying to eat while talking at the same time. 'Even in *Don Quixote*.'

I sat up. Spanish literature was virtually founded on *Don Quixote*, Cervantes regarded as a kind of Spanish Shakespeare. Was there a Moorish influence in the great book?

The famous story about the old man tilting at windmills because he believed them to be giants was a simple multilingual pun, Pedro explained. The windmill symbolized the *emir al-mu'minin* – the title of the fanatical leader of the fundamentalist Almohads who had once ruled Al-Andalus. It meant 'leader of the faithful', an epithet often used in an Islamic context, but Spaniards who didn't understand Arabic well had garbled the name, dubbing the dreaded fanatic *miralmolín*.

'*Miralmolín*,' Pedro repeated, an expectant look in his eye. 'What does that sound like to you . . . ?'

He paused, waiting for me to fill in. I was still trying to keep up with him as his conversation veered from one subject to the next. I turned the word over in my mind, trying to hear its supposed homonym.

'*Mira el molino* – Look at the windmill,' I said with a start, Cervantes' play on words suddenly becoming clear.

'Exactly,' he said. 'Look at the windmill.'

In one brief episode of his lengthy book – the scene which most people remember – Cervantes drew neatly on both Moorish and Christian Spanish cultures, and the in-between world which the two had once combined to create. Don Quixote wasn't charging at imaginary monsters. He was poking fun at fundamentalists.

A whole new layer of meaning was emerging as Pedro spoke.

'Cervantes himself admits a Moorish influence,' he went on. 'The story was told to him by an old Morisco translating into Spanish from a book by the Arab author Cide Hamete Benengeli. It's a made-up Arab name,' he said, waving his hand dismissively. 'But it's Cervantes' coded way of saying where some of his material comes from. Remember, he spent five years as a captive in Algiers. There are even Sufi jokes in the *Quixote*.'

I drank some more tea as I took this all in: the

mother of all Western novels owed much, it seemed, to Al-Andalus. Cervantes had been writing as Moorish Spain was in its death throes – the years just before and after the expulsion of the Moriscos. The country would still have been soaked in the influence of the old Arab culture. Except that few people mentioned this when they talked about the book. I suspected that Cervantes, who was writing as the Inquisition was at its peak, would have had to disguise some of the sources of his inspiration: fundamentalism, this time dressed in Christian clothes, was once again taking over men's minds.

There was a pause, and as though gauging this was the right moment to say something, Zine started to speak.

'Muslim culture in Al-Andalus was the most advanced of its day,' he said. 'That's what Jasie is looking for, I think. Although I don't know how much he will find. But in the past, yes, of course. We gave you music, poetry, medicine, mathematics . . .'

'And toothpaste,' Pedro said. 'Don't forget that.' And he told us how the Moors used to make it from boiled walnut root mixed with cloves and coriander.

'They used to rub it on their teeth like this.' He pushed a finger into the side of his mouth and laughed like a child.

'But that was all a long time ago,' Zine said. 'Spain is not a Moorish country now. Come to Morocco and see a Moorish country. This is Europe. There's more money, fewer *bidonvilles*.'

Pedro and I had both been to Morocco, as well as other Middle Eastern countries. The differences were obvious, even in basic things. There was a far more visible culture gap in the half-hour ferry journey from

Tarifa to Tangier than there was in a two-day drive from Seville to Paris, for example. You didn't see camels grazing in fields or men in jellabas and fezes anywhere in Europe. Yet it was precisely the less visible legacy of the Moors that I wanted to find.

'Excuse me,' Pedro said, and he got up to go and answer the telephone ringing inside the house.

It was probably foolish, I thought, for two Westerners to try to convince a Moroccan that Spain was still Moorish. For Zine the foreignness of the place, and his foreignness in it, was all too clear. The police, if they found him, would make sure of that.

'You should go to Murcia tomorrow,' Pedro said, coming back from the house and sitting between us. 'See the city where Ibn al-Arabi was born. Nothing remains of his house, but something of his presence in the air, perhaps.'

'*Baraka*,' said Zine. It was an Arabic word meaning something like 'blessing' or 'good luck'.

'Exactly,' said Pedro. For a moment it seemed they were on the same wavelength. '*Tabarak Allah alik*.'

And the water in his hookah bubbled glob glob glob as he drew in another lungful of honey-scented smoke.

THE ROAD TO
ALMERÍA

'Your friend Pedro is *ahmaq*. A bit crazy, I think.'

The roadside café was decorated with dark-green flock wallpaper and filled with truck drivers and a group of bin-men eating three-course lunches. In Spain they say that when on the road you should stop off where the most lorries are parked – that way you know you'll eat well. Something which, having been brought up in England, it took me a while to grasp.

'You may be right,' I said. 'But he's given me some clues.'

Taking Pedro's advice, we had driven to Murcia the following day, through a flat, hazy landscape dotted with cuboid earth-coloured farms and randomly placed palm trees lifting from the ground like shooting stars. Large areas were little more than scrubland, while every few hundred yards a new estate stood half built and empty, a new scar in the semi-desert: with their thin walls and cheap materials, they looked as if they would be falling down within a decade or two. It was a cowboy builder's paradise.

We had spent the morning in the city itself, wandering the narrow streets of the old quarter. As Pedro had said, there was nothing to show of Ibn al-Arabi's birthplace. The cathedral, however, built on the site of the old mosque, was the last resting place of the heart of King Alfonso X 'the Wise'. Alfonso had been an enthusiastic admirer of Moorish learning and culture, and commissioned a large number of books to be translated from Arabic into Castillian Spanish. He was also a lover of another great Moorish import into Europe: chess. Originating from an ancient Indian game, chess was adopted by the Persians, who passed it on to the Arabs, who then brought it to Spain. In most European languages the name 'chess' was derived from the Persian 'shah', meaning king. The Spanish *ajedrez* and the Portuguese *xadrez* both came from the Arabic name for the game: *al-shatranj*. The castle, or rook, was known in Spanish as the *roque* and came from the Persian *rukh*. The bishop was called the *alfil* and came from the Arabic for elephant, *al-fil*. Although records of chess being played in Spain date from 1008, Alfonso wrote the first description of the game in a European language in the thirteenth century, complete with miniatures showing players mostly wearing Arab clothes.

Alfonso was also responsible for a great collection of poetry known as the *Cantigas de Santa María*. Although written in Galician dialect, the poetic forms used were almost entirely *zajals* and *muwashshahs* – styles unique to Moorish Spain, having been developed centuries earlier by the poet Ibn Quzman. Both these forms later developed into the Spanish *villancico* – used for all kinds of Christian poetry, particularly Christmas carols.

We moved on from Murcia, pausing for lunch as we pushed southwards into the barren mountains of

Almería. Zine stared at the waitress as she leant over to place two plates of *arroz al horno* and anchovies in vinegar on the table, her tight black trousers distracting him for a moment from the TV, with its talk of ever-closer war. A year before, in this same bar, I had first seen images of the suicide attacks on the World Trade Center, stopping off for a drink as I drove south to Andalusia. It had seemed surreal then, watching this dramatic and horrifying event take place thousands of miles away while sitting in the middle of a rocky desert, the only sound the passing of an occasional car on the empty road outside. Now, though, the images had become as familiar as a fizzy-pop commercial.

'The CIA and Mossad were behind this,' Zine said, pointing at the screen as the waitress walked away. 'Some Frenchman – Thierry Meyssan – has written a book about it explaining everything. They needed it as an excuse to attack Afghanistan and now Iraq.'

Like many Arabs, it seemed he was ready to believe the most complicated and far-fetched rumours, especially if you could fit Mossad in there somewhere.

'Of course. This is American imperialism. How come all the Jews were told to leave the Twin Towers before the attacks?'

'Were they?' I found these theories hard to take.

'They want to control the oil.'

I was living in Alexandria during the protracted build-up to the previous Gulf War, and had grown increasingly alarmed, then ever more cynical, as the various ideas about what was going to happen to us all became more and more exaggerated every day. The lack of any decent local media coverage meant it was all too easy to speculate in an information vacuum.

'Revolution will break out in Jordan ... Scuds carrying chemical weapons will overshoot Israel and land in the Delta ... Libya and Sudan will simultaneously invade Egypt.' Or my personal favourite: 'Mossad have mined the Aswan dam and will blow it up, flooding the country and wiping it out in only seven hours.' Or nine hours, or eleven, depending on who was repeating this secret to you.

'As far as I can see,' I said, 'everyone's talking about hijacked planes, but the real hijacking here is of Islam.'

'Islam?'

'Al-Qa'ida says it's an Islamic group, but suicide is forbidden, *haram*.'

'And by dying as a martyr you go straight to heaven.'

It was the usual argument: the attackers were 'fighters' losing their lives rather than taking them. Committing suicide in a way that killed other people as well was somehow acceptable and even rewarded, where solitary self-murder was not.

'They're not the first people to think that nonsense,' I said.

In the ninth century, a group of some fifty Christian extremists had been killed by the Moorish rulers and became known as the Martyrs of Córdoba. They got it into their heads that living under Muslim rather than Christian rule, albeit tolerated by the authorities, was somehow a bad thing, and decided to raise their profile by seeking audiences with the emir and openly insulting Muhammad and Islam in front of him. At first the emir dismissed them as harmless lunatics, but when they persisted he gave them what they wanted and had them decapitated for blasphemy. Other Christians were appalled by their co-religionists' behaviour and condemned them, but some applauded their attempt to emulate those martyred at the hands of the Romans.

'They said exactly the same things as this lot today. It's the same madness, just a different religion.'

He grinned.

'Muslims are supposed to be tolerant of Christians and Jews,' I said. 'They're protected people – *dhimmis*.'

'Only when they live in Islamic countries. Like Morocco: we have many Jews living there.'

The waitress returned with a bottle of wine and some lemonade to mix together. *Tinto de verano*, they called it: summer red wine.

'*Allah*.' Zine looked up at her, his eyebrows arched and a pleading expression on his face.

'*Hola*,' she said, smiling back at him.

'I'm interested in when cultures like Islam and the West come together,' I said. It took a moment for Zine's concentration to return to the table. Smiling seductively as she looked down at him, the waitress finally walked away; for a second I'd almost thought she was going to sit down and have lunch with us.

'What about the times when they seemed to get on?' I said. 'What happened then?'

'You're a romantic. That's history,' he laughed, looking back towards the bar where the girl was passing on a drinks order to a man in a stained white shirt. She glanced over at our table and smiled again before turning her head, flirtation lighting up her eyes.

'We study Al-Andalus like you study – I don't know what . . . the Romans and the Greeks. Interesting, but it's over.'

'We should stop looking at what's usual and start trying to understand the unusual,' I said. 'It happened right here, right where we're sitting: Moors, Christians and Jews lived together and created a great civilization.'

'Of course. That's what Pedro said. But what do you want? You think you can re-create Córdoba just by driving around Spain with a *moro* in the passenger seat?'

I placed my fork down slowly and stared at him. He laughed.

'OK. Don't get angry. It's just a joke.'

Cheeky bugger, I thought.

As our conversation dried up, I noticed that the group of bin-men at the table next to us had a North African in their midst. He sat quietly near the leader, eating hungrily and sniggering at the mildly insulting comments being made about him by the others. He and Zine were aware of one another, but some sort of group pressure was at work, and the man's will to be accepted by the bunch of red-eyed alcoholics who'd become his fellow workers made him ignore his compatriot just a few feet away. Struggling to become one of 'them'. Although the difference was more cultural than anything else: the head dustbin-man could easily have just flown in from Istanbul, with his heavy skin, thick black moustache and ill-fitting toupee.

The waitress was at our table again, this time to clear away. Zine handed her our plates, pretending to drop them just as he passed them over. She laughed with him as he opened his eyes wide in pretend shock and panic.

'Do you want to give me a hand?' she asked. Most of her lipstick had smudged, leaving a dark border at the edges where she'd drawn with a liner.

'Just the bill, please,' I said.

Zine lingered over her football-shaped buttocks as she walked back towards the kitchen. I'd seen more advanced flirting at the reptile house at London Zoo.

'She likes me,' he said with a victorious grin.

'You seem to have forgotten Lucía pretty fast.'

'Lucía wanted some fun. I gave it to her.' He paused for a minute. 'Look, you're always going on about Moors and Christians, Islam and the West, how things were better in the past. Well, I'm doing my own bit for racial harmony.'

'How?'

He laughed.

'There'll be no more racism when these girls find they've got a bit of Moor in them.'

And before I could say anything, he got up from the table and walked calmly towards the back door through which the waitress had just passed.

ALMERÍA

*I*t was overcast when we reached the top of the Alcazaba, and a chill breeze blew in from the unusually grey Mediterranean. You didn't often see it so stripped of colour and there was a sense of unease about it, as though searching deep down for the blues and purples that it usually shone forth with the light of the sun.

We climbed up the battlements of the old Moorish walls to stare out at the city of Almería below.

'Look, this is just like the castles in Morocco,' Zine mumbled angrily as we walked through horseshoe archways past suspicious-looking security guards wearing mirrored sunglasses and standing incongruously among the rose bushes. He was still annoyed that the woman back in the tourist office had insisted the buildings were all Spanish.

'Interested in *lo moro*?' she said when I asked for information. 'They built everything in brick. *We're* the ones restoring it. Now all these North Africans are coming to settle here saying it's all theirs. I don't know what'll become of us, I really don't.'

At least the black and tabby kittens now rubbing

themselves against our legs didn't care where you came from.

The Alcazaba was Almería's main tourist attraction: a giant fortress that stood on the hills above the city, built in the tenth century by the greatest caliph of Al-Andalus – Abd al-Rahman III, who turned what had been a simple harbour watchtower into a major metropolis and flourishing port. Not quite an Alhambra – no carved wooden ceilings or Arabesques decorating the walls – it was, nonetheless, an imposing place that overlooked the run-down streets below like a reminder of greater times.

On our walk up through the city that morning we saw an elderly one-eyed woman dressed in black sitting in the doorway of her flat cube-house, pulling back the metal chains that kept the flies out in order to spit into the gutter just a yard away from her feet. Although the houses were only a hundred years old, the design had barely changed since Moorish times. There was a gloominess about the place, though, as if it was just half a generation away from becoming a ghost town. Once-bustling, winding streets, full of donkeys, children and workshops like the northern Moroccan towns it reminded me of, were now empty and barren. Below the castle walls, a stone's throw from the nearest houses, car-wrecks decorated the dry hillside, given, I imagined, one last moment of glory as they rolled spectacularly down into the valley before they were left to rot. The place smelt of sand and diesel.

'Moroccan ship,' Zine said simply as he looked down at the white and green FerriMaroc vessel moving out from the harbour in front of us. A pillar of black smoke rose from its funnel into the still, humid air.

'Homesick?' I said.

He'd been downbeat all day. I'd offered to put him up at the *pensión* I was staying at, but he'd refused, boasting instead that he'd find a warm bed somewhere in the city. His brief but astounding conquest of the waitress at the roadside café seemed to have given him some confidence about his luck with Spanish girls. I hadn't minded – apart from having to wait in the car for twenty minutes before he came running out from the back smothering a grin on his face – but I wasn't sure if it was going to be a practical way of dealing with the question of board and lodging, as he seemed to be imagining, all the time. And then there was Lucía: it was none of my business, I told myself, but I assumed that that relationship had ended back in Valencia.

Now, though, standing on the castle battlements gazing out to sea, he looked tired, unshaven and melancholy, and I had the strong impression he'd slept rough. Perhaps the girls of a port city like Almería weren't so easily impressed by tales of lost orphans far from home.

'I want nothing more than to go back to Morocco,' he said, slouching his shoulders as he leant out over the wall. 'Smell the incense in the markets, hear people speaking Arabic again, see my friends.'

It was the first time I had seen him like this. Something had happened the night before to knock the hopefulness out of him, and I cursed myself for not insisting that he stay in the hotel with me. Yet I sensed that his dependence on me was beginning to grate on him. If he could find something else on the way, he would probably take it: I'd made a promise, yet he was free to do what he wanted.

'I would go. But . . .' He trailed off.

The sound of trickling water started behind us as the fountains were switched on. I turned my back to the sea and looked up at the sloping rose gardens, wood pigeons cooing gently from the trees. An Andalusi poet, Ibn Hazm, had once written a book of love poetry called *The Pigeon's Necklace*. From eleventh-century Spain, his sophisticated romanticism had spread north, influencing the troubadours and the emergence of courtly love in France and England.

> When I leave your side my steps
> Are like those of a condemned man.
> To reach you, I run like the full moon
> Crossing the confines of the sky.
> But to leave you, I move slowly
> As the highest stars.

This new, more refined and poetic view of human relationships had quickly caught on: they said a Christian prisoner once held in the Alcazaba of Almería had thrown himself to his death from one of the towers after falling in love with a Moorish slave girl. The girl had tried to help him escape, but their plan had been discovered, causing him to take his own life. She later died from a broken heart.

'Perhaps you should go back,' I said.

'*In sha' Allah.*' Then, lifting his head and turning to me with a flat smile, he added, '*Ojalá.*'

I grinned and placed my hand on his shoulder. Despite his defeated air, he could still make gentle fun of my obsession – *ojalá* being the Spanish derivation of *in sha' Allah*.

'The most difficult thing,' he said, lifting himself

straight and turning towards me, 'is facing everyone at home. I can't return without any money. You think I can turn up with tales of farm work and those bastards who kept us locked up, and not bring back a single euro, a single dollar? It's all shit. There, here. Wherever. I need work, money. Here there's no work; there there's no money.'

'You seem to be having a good time, though,' I said.

'We have girls in Morocco, too,' he said. 'Pretty girls.'

'So?'

'OK, so here it's easier to go to bed with them. But there are girls like that in Morocco too, if you want them. You know. You are just like me – standing there passing judgement, but you left home too. You have a foreign girl, not English. It's different.'

It was sometimes easy to forget we were both foreigners in this country, but each saw the other as less of an outsider than himself: in my eyes because he was Moorish, and for him because I was a Westerner. To me, Almería felt almost like an extension of Morocco, a foothold across the Mediterranean. Ferries with Arabic writing on them steamed in and out of the port; there were Moroccan tea-houses on the esplanade, a mosque in a first-floor flat, and North Africans crowding the streets heading down to the sea front. Yet it was also the least welcoming place I had ever come across in the whole time I had been in Spain, with its edgy atmosphere and empty landscape stripped bare. Nothing in this far south-eastern corner of the peninsula felt familiar to me; there was nothing I could identify with or warm to. It was Spain, and clearly Moorish, yet none of the things that normally appealed to me about Spain were evident, as though some vital element I had not yet identified was missing, noticeable only by its absence.

But Zine, so close as we were to Morocco, gazed mournfully out to sea, and felt as isolated as I did.

'This is not my home; it never can be,' he said. 'Perhaps for you, but here I am foreign.'

As we'd passed through villages on our way to Almería the day before, we'd seen headscarf-wearing women sitting on the steps of their houses, peeling almonds as they chattered in low voices and turning their faces away modestly as we'd slowed down to look. The faces in this part of Spain were dark, and many men who passed us in the street had widely set-apart eyes, like so many Berbers. In the countryside, agricultural co-operatives known as *alhondigas* worked the land, their name derived from an old Arabic word for corn exchange. At almost every turn there was the evidence I needed. But for Zine it was still, and always would be, Spain.

I too felt foreign here, though, a country that looked up to and simultaneously disdained other cultures: from my hair colour and features it was obvious I was an outsider – not even from the north, where you often saw lighter skins and blue-green eyes. Accident of birth, childhood associations, being comfortable with what you knew – did 'belonging' ever account to more than this, though? We were both connected to, yet dislocated from, the land we were crossing.

'Let's go.' Zine pulled himself away from the battlements and headed up the slope towards the keep, scuffing his shoes on the steps as he walked between decorative terracotta gutters. I stayed for a few minutes more, scanning the sea.

* * *

'I've discovered something for you,' he said, coming back to find me not much further on.

I'd been watching the castle cats in operation. When first you saw them they quickly won your sympathy – all battered and skinny, with half-closed eyes as though almost blind. Who could refuse to pass on whatever crumbs he had in his pocket to such unfortunate creatures? But if you continued to watch them, once the tourists had walked on they quickly transformed into lively, healthy bundles of energy, racing up and down the hill in the undergrowth in search of playmates. A skill passed on from generation to generation, perhaps, and far more convincing than many of the human beggars I'd seen.

'What's that?' I asked.

'This was a major silk and textiles centre under the Moors,' he said. 'I've just been talking to one of the gardeners.'

'*You've* been talking to the gardeners?'

'Yes. I thought they might have some work for me. But the man's an idiot – thought I was some visiting professor from Casablanca, or something. So he starts telling me about the history and the Moors. Ha, ha.'

'What else did he say?'

'Not much.'

'See those?' I said, pointing to the cats now lazing underneath an oleander tree. 'They're tabbies. "Tabby" comes from the name of an old quarter of Baghdad where they made striped cloth, which used to be imported into Europe through this very port. Hence the name for stripy cats.'

'OK. Well, I can tell you where the name Almería comes from.'

'Where?' I said. Our unexpected sparring match was

bringing the colour back into his face, and his voice rose into his usual high-pitched sing-song. For the first time he seemed less than dismissive of my pet subject.

'*Al-miraya* – the mirror.'

The usual etymology given was that it came from the Arabic for watchtower – *al-mariyya*. But at that moment this new origin for the city's name seemed more apt: grey as the sky was, the sea below had an almost silvery, mirror-like feeling to it.

'There, you see?' I said with a laugh. 'It's a reflection of Morocco, of North Africa.'

'A reflection,' he said. 'Not the real thing.'

CHAPIZ

'*S*pain is essentially a Latin country. There's far too much emphasis today on Al-Andalus and the Moors.'

We were sitting in a 500-year-old Moorish house in Granada's Albaicín quarter, the view from Camilo's window dominated by the Alhambra on the hill opposite.

'When I was a child, at school we hardly studied the Arab period of Spanish history at all. Now, though, they've forgotten about the Romans.'

I was surprised by Camilo's statement. I had expected a professor of Arabic history to be, if anything, a fan of his country's Moorish past. But his comment reminded me of a number of other Arabists I'd met, who seemed to develop a curious hostility towards their chosen subject the further into their books they buried themselves. Like paparazzi, who always spoke with a peculiar venom when interviewed about the people they spent their lives taking pictures of.

Camilo Alvarez de Morales was a former classmate of Pedro; they had studied Arabic together back in the sixties. Today, he held a post at the Escuela de

Estudios Arabes, one of the most important centres of Islamic studies in the country. The building itself was an important piece of Granada's Moorish past – the Casa del Chapiz sat at the far end of the Albaicín on the edge of the Sacromonte, the traditional Gypsy area, and was one of the oldest houses in the city. Built by an influential sixteenth-century Morisco merchant – Lorenzo el Chapiz – it was renovated in the early twentieth century by Leopoldo Torres Balbás, the same man who restored the Alhambra. In many ways it felt like a miniature version of the palace across the valley, with its delicate columns, tranquil gardens and Arabesques decorating high archways. A long rect-angular pool flanked by myrtle bushes and covered in lilies was the centrepiece of the old courtyard below Camilo's office.

We sat inside, protected from the midday heat and humidity. Camilo, grey haired and moustached, appeared rather formal sitting behind his dark heavy desk, and a row of books propped on one side created a kind of double barrier between us as I sat on a chair opposite. It felt more like an interview than a chat with a friend of a friend with a common interest.

'Some people talk about the end of Al-Andalus – the conquest of Granada – as a kind of national tragedy. But I'll tell you what it would be like here today if Ferdinand and Isabel had never taken the city – it would be like Morocco.'

He didn't mean it as a compliment.

In his view, the Nasrids, the reigning dynasty of Moorish Granada, had essentially been decadent rulers. The Alhambra might have been a magnificent palace, but it was built at the same time as the European Renaissance was getting off the ground.

The Moors in Spain by this point were in decline, and scientifically Granada had nothing to offer its Christian neighbours.

I shuffled in my seat. Technically, perhaps, Moorish Granada was merely equal or inferior to late-medieval Spain, but the Alhambra was one of the most magical places I had ever visited, with a certain rare power to it. I wasn't sure if anywhere in Christian Europe quite matched it – at best a handful of Gothic cathedrals came close. How could a culture that produced such a masterpiece be dismissed as merely 'decadent'?

When I asked him if Spain still resembled a Moorish country, his answer was dismissive.

'We absorbed elements from the Arabs, but there wasn't this marvellous co-existence between Muslims and Christians that's been romanticized by some historians. We're Europeans – Latins and Visigoths.'

I noticed his use of the word 'we', but continued with my next question, as much as anything to see his reaction.

'You don't think of yourself as having Moorish blood at all?'

'No,' he said without a pause. 'I study the history of Al-Andalus as an outsider.'

'Like a biologist looking down his microscope,' I said.

'Yes. Objectively. Scientifically.'

Speaking to him was a stark contrast to being with Pedro, his old university friend. I couldn't help feeling, though, that much was lost when you only looked at something down the end of a long metal tube, as he was proud to admit. Microscopes were all very well for seeing small things in detail, but how could an academic talk about the smell of a city, or expressions on faces, body language or the flavour of food? Or was it that, as Zine had said and now Camilo was suggesting, I was just a romantic?

Feeling my way around the conversation, looking for a chink in the wall-like armour he seemed to have placed around himself, I asked Camilo about the mosque I'd seen earlier that morning being built on the crest of the Albaicín hill. Overlooking the Darro valley, it sat directly opposite the Alhambra.

'No one knows who's behind it,' he said with a note of annoyance in his voice. 'I think the imam is Scottish.' I laughed, but he didn't appear to find it funny. 'Some say Libyans are paying for it, but we don't know. Sometimes the money runs out and it stays as it is for a few months, then the builders come back and it's all go again. But its position on top of the Albaicín is a bit . . .' He paused.

'Provocative?' I said.

'Yes. It's a statement. There are a lot more Arabs here now than there were, say, ten years ago.'

I had noticed this as well. It was common to see veiled women on almost every street in the centre of town – a rarity only six or seven years beforehand.

'What happens is Spanish converts to Islam marry Moroccans and then the whole family comes over. The numbers are increasing.'

He looked uneasy. It seemed the professor of Arabic was not entirely pleased that Arabs were becoming more numerous in his home town.

'We dedicate ourselves here to studying medieval history, though,' he said quickly. 'We're not concerned with what's happening today.' It appeared we'd taken a wrong turn in our conversation.

It seemed typical of the academic approach: a whole

125

culture reduced to some minute aspect of the Arabic language, a forgotten poet, or a period of history buried in dusty books and under sand dunes. Very few seemed to have any living contact with the Arab world, and you wondered if some of them could even hold a proper conversation with an ordinary Arab, or whether, like the dons at Oxford who'd taught me, they studiously avoided ever having to speak the language. There were notable uncommon exceptions, but I often wondered if an academic environment might not actually be unsuitable for what it purported to be about: the collection and passing on of knowledge.

If 'dreaming' Oxford seemed slightly detached from reality, Camilo's Escuela was more like a fortress: high walls closing it off from the outside, a tiny plaque on the door stating what actually went on there. I'd walked past it scores of times on previous visits to the area and had never realized what it was. And now I hadn't gained entry without an interrogation from a suspicious woman at the entrance lodge and a severe quizzing from one of the professors I'd bumped into while finding my way to Camilo's office. All this despite having a previously arranged appointment. It felt as if I'd falsely gained access to an exclusive gentlemen's club.

'Perhaps you'd like to look around?'

Camilo stood up, much smaller than he'd looked behind his desk, and we walked out onto the wooden gallery that ran around two sides of the old patio. A gardener was slowly sweeping up dead leaves from around the pool.

'This house is a *carmen*,' he said. Walking around the Albaicín, you noticed many houses were called Carmen This or Carmen That.

'A carmen is when you have both a garden *and* an orchard,' he continued. 'The word comes from the Arabic *karm*, or vineyard.'

So even the name of Spain's most famous femme fatale had an Arabic etymology. Although perhaps it was little more than the simple absorption of another element of Moorish culture by an essentially Latin society, as Camilo had argued.

He filled me in on more details about the renovation of the house, pointing out stucco work on the archways and niches in the walls, but as he spoke I found myself pondering the fact that ideas about history were subject to fashion just as much as anything else. Depending on who you listened to, Al-Andalus was responsible for all that was good or all that was bad about the place.

'Without Islam,' one Spanish Arabist had written in the late 1920s, 'Spain would have followed the same course as France, Germany, Italy and England: and to judge by what was actually accomplished through the centuries, Spain might have led the way. But it was not to be. Islam conquered the whole of the Peninsula, distorted the destinies of Iberia and allotted to it a different part in the tragi-comedy of history . . . which proved extremely expensive to Spain.'

Perhaps. Yet the author of these words, Claudio Sánchez Albornoz, had been a perfect example – albeit in name alone – of the marriage between Moorish and Christian in Spain: his surname made up of the Visigothic 'son of Sancho' and the Arabic 'the man with the burnous'.

On the other side were people who stressed the importance of the Moors and Jews in the development of the very concept of 'Spain'. Pedro was an example of this school, but its most famous advocate had been Américo Castro, whose ideas Sánchez Albornoz had attacked.

Academics who denied or belittled the Moorish influence on Spain and Europe often did so in a way that seemed to defy common sense. They claimed that the polite Spanish form for 'you', *usted*, had nothing to do with the Arabic honorific *ustadh*, and originated solely from a shortening of *vuestra merced*, a formal mode of address used in the past. Or they denied any Moorish roots for the troubadour movement, despite clear similarities with certain Arabic poetic themes (chivalry was virtually invented in pre-Islamic Arabia) and the fact that the Arabic verb *tarab* and its variants mean 'to make music', 'to sing', 'to fill with joy', or 'to move with music'. Just add the Spanish active-participle suffix -*ador* and you get 'troubadour'. But no. Sometimes you got the impression the Inquisition had never actually ended.

To claim that Spain was basically Roman seemed almost perverse: its capital city had an Arabic name: *majrit*, from *majra*, meaning water channel; the highest mountain on the mainland, Mulhacén, whose snowy cap we could see in the distance above Granada, had an Arabic name; its most famous river, the Guadalquivir, had an Arabic name (*al-wadi al-kabir* - the big river); what was fast turning into its national dish, paella, had strong Middle Eastern over-tones, and the word gazpacho probably came from Spanish Arabic; its signature music, flamenco, had some of its origins in North African musical forms. Perhaps the only emblematic thing in Spain that didn't come from the Moors was bullfighting.

Some of the formality of earlier finally dropped

away as Camilo and I said our goodbyes. The small old man, who had seemed so stiff in his office, shook my hand warmly, placing his left hand on my elbow, and asked after Pedro, smiling for the first time since I'd arrived. It was a shame we hadn't conducted the whole meeting walking around this ancient house, I thought. His huge desk had seemed like a fence, and I was sure it had had an effect on our conversation.

'Pedro is a dear friend of mine,' he said. 'I'm very glad he sent you.'

It felt a sudden way to end it. I would have liked to ask him to have lunch with me, or something, just to show that we were finally beginning to make contact. But the circumstances, perhaps, or the distance that elderly Granadinos always maintain with people they've just met, made it impossible. There was a certain darkness and seriousness there that reminded me of particularly religious Arab cities like Fez, or the Al-Azhar district of Cairo. Perhaps there was more of the Arab in him than he cared to admit. With one last look across the valley to the Alhambra, framed by the cypress trees shooting out of the earth like green fountains, I turned to leave.

MUHAMMAD

*T*hree days had passed since I'd last seen Zine. Again I'd offered to put him up, and again he'd refused, unbowed by his failure in Almería, and he'd taken off into the unknown city to find his own way. It had come as something of a relief, but now I wanted to find him and had come looking in the dozens of Moroccan *teterías* that had sprung up on the Calderería Nueva, one of the narrow cobblestone streets that led from modern Granada into the labyrinth of the Albaicín. A mini bazaar was in the process of being created here, with shop after shop being turned over to selling crystal lanterns, brightly coloured striped cloths, octagonal wooden tables with inlaid Arabesques, and brass coffee pots. Almost everyone working here was Moroccan or Algerian, it seemed: men dressed like Zine in jeans and trainers, with skinny sloping shoulders, and others wearing more traditional robes – green or black jellabas with Islamic white skullcaps. I'd caught sight of one moving slowly and amiably from shopkeeper to shopkeeper as he worked his way up the street, receiving warm handshakes and just slightly too much respect from each one as he exchanged a few words before moving on. I'd seen this before scores of times in Middle Eastern countries – the fawning behaviour reserved for imams and others high up in the – usually religious – hierarchy: all smiles and warmth for someone who had far too much power and say in other people's lives. Politicians were similarly treated, but they usually didn't go around with the same aura of holiness. For a religion that officially was supposed not to have priests, only a direct relationship between God and man, in many Islamic countries there was a very clear spiritual pecking order.

I felt slightly uncomfortable about the scene I was witnessing, but I wasn't quite sure why. In somewhere like Egypt I might not even have noticed, so common was it. But I remembered an incident in a minibus once, driving from Tel Aviv to Jerusalem. One of the passengers had been an ultra-orthodox Jew, a grim, humourless-looking man who insisted on sitting in the front next to the driver, forcing the woman who was already there to move to the back. Just a few minutes into the ride he turned to the driver and insisted that the pop-music station on the radio be switched off. The driver complied, albeit reluctantly. When we got to Jerusalem, however, and our party-pooping companion had been dropped off in an area outside the centre of town, the radio immediately went back on and the driver launched into a lengthy public tirade against the religious conservatives. There was no way he was letting any more on his bus, he shouted to us all in the back. A vain protest, perhaps, but it showed just a small degree of defiance against the fanatics – something I had never come across so openly among contemporary Muslims. You might find the same sentiments privately, but there was also an unspoken worry that you never knew who might be listening. The hard-liners were steadily taking over through fear.

'Hello, Jasie? I'm Muhammad.'

A tall, white-skinned Spaniard with a felt-black beard and heavy eyebrows thrust his hand towards me. He sat down in front of me and nodded to the waitress, who quickly brought over some mint tea.

'I'm a Muslim,' he said, pouring himself a cup through a tiny metal sieve. 'Muhammad López. Your friend Zine said you wanted to meet me.'

I had never heard of him, nor had I expressed a desire to do anything of the sort, but I assumed that Zine thought he was doing me a favour, and yes, this could be interesting – a Spanish convert to Islam. Where was Zine right now and how did he know where I was?

'My parents gave me the name Francisco, but I changed it, of course, when I became a Muslim,' Muhammad said. There was a coldness in his round eyes, as though he were used to encounters like this, and having to explain his faith to scoffers and the curious.

From a choice of thousands of Arabic names, you couldn't really give him top marks for imagination, plumping for the most obviously Islamic name of the lot, but I decided to suspend judgement for the time being, trying to control my usual unease with anyone who'd converted to anything.

He'd become a Muslim five years earlier when he met his Moroccan wife, he told me.

'So you did it for love?' I said.

'That was how I originally came to Islam,' he said. If a non-Muslim man wanted to marry a Muslim woman

134

he had to convert first, he explained. That way the children were brought up as Muslims too.

'Do you have children?'

'No. I have a low sperm count.'

Conversion to Islam, I was happy to see, had not done away with the common Spanish trait of speaking with utter frankness about bodily functions. For a moment I felt sorry for him.

'But I have a new family now,' he went on, forcing the burning hot tea down his throat. 'All Muslims are my family.'

I wasn't sure I really wanted to hear too much about brotherly love at this hour in the morning, but his views on being a Spanish Muslim chimed with all the thinking I'd been doing. What was so unusual about being a Spanish Muslim? Many Spaniards had been Muslims at one time. But Muhammad felt that Spain itself was uncomfortable with people like him, despite the fact that he believed himself to be perhaps even more Spanish than the rest. Spain, in his eyes, was never conquered, but integrated into the Islamic world.

It seemed clear that he and I would share quite a few ideas about Spanish history and the role Muslims played in it: not the military imposition of a foreign culture from abroad, but more a cultural phenomenon, where Spain, intellectually, artistically, religiously and commercially, became part of the Islamic sphere of influence. There was, however, a slight vehemence in his tone which I didn't warm to, and perhaps too much readiness to refer to non-Muslim Spaniards as 'them'.

I wondered if he identified himself with the Moriscos, the Moors who were forced to convert to Christianity after the fall of Granada.

'Yes. With the Moriscos, with the Arabs, the Berbers, the Syrians, but also the native peoples of the peninsula, all of whom were once united under the religion of Islam.'

This was pushing the image of racial harmony a bit far, I thought. Berbers and Arabs, co-religionists in Al-Andalus, had been at loggerheads for decades over who got the best plots of land. Despite the egalitarianism of Islam, Arabs could be very disdainful of other races, and it showed in the rebellions and internal social divisions that had dogged much of the early history of Moorish Spain. But it was interesting, after my conversations with Zine trying to defend the country's Moorishness, that I was now on the other foot, finding fault with Muhammad's over-enthusiasm for the Islamic period.

'What is happening now is an aberration,' Muhammad continued. 'The West wants conflict with Islam; it needs an enemy. People think Al-Qa'ida was behind September the Eleventh.' He gave a joyless laugh. 'It's quite obvious the Americans did it. They needed excuses to impose themselves on the Middle East. Islam is a religion of peace.'

There was a kind of blind certainty in his manner that I recognized from other intensely religious people, and a dismissiveness, as though you hadn't a hope of reaching the heights of his understanding.

It was depressing to see how polarized opinions were over the September attacks. First Zine and now Muhammad, like so many other Arabs and Muslims, positioned on one side, and Westerners on the other. As though that in itself marked a dividing line any future conflicts would be based upon. The centre ground was increasingly depopulated.

Having seen the mosque being built on the Albaicín hill, the increasing numbers of veiled women, teahouses and Moroccan shops around, an idea flitted into my head that someone or some group out there – perhaps Muhammad, in front of me now – was secretly planning on retaking the city for Islam. It was crazy, perhaps. But in today's climate I couldn't put it past some lunatic somewhere to want to 'avenge' the loss of Granada to the Christians five centuries earlier: a romanticized defeat of a former Islamic jewel that appealed to many Arabs' yearning for a lost Golden Age.

'Do you think . . .' I hesitated. 'Should Spain become a Muslim country once more?'

'We have no problem with Christians or Jews. Israel is another matter. But it was Christians who threw out the Muslims and the Jews from Spain. Muslims never harmed anyone.'

'What about the massacre of the Jewish population here in Granada by the Moors in 1066?' I asked.

'A one-off. It was a political struggle. The Jews were running the place. Nothing to do with their religion or race. As I said, Islam is a religion of peace. *Salam.*'

I decided to move things back to more personal matters, asking him how his family had reacted when he converted.

It hadn't been easy. His mother was unhappy about his conversion. She felt he'd let down his father, who had died when Muhammad was only a teenager. None of his protestations about Spain's Muslim heritage washed with her, and now he only saw her a couple of times a year in their home town of Cáceres. Muhammad had moved to Granada because of his wife, who worked helping immigrants, but for him Granada was also a city of special importance, a city for converts, the last Moorish city to fall.

I asked if he knew anything about the new mosque on the top of the Albaicín.

'No,' he said vaguely. 'Nothing to do with us. That's a different group. I'm not sure if they're Libyan, or something.'

He sat back on his wooden stool and took his eyes off me for a second to look around the room, as though to indicate he'd had enough. I felt relief at not being under his piercing gaze. Strange how no one knew about the mosque, though.

We stepped out together into the street, where the sweet smell of fried cinnamon cakes filled the air. Virginia creeper fell over the wall of a nearby carmen like the long greasy hair of a teenager. The Arabic word *al-huriyya* – freedom – was spray-painted on the building opposite. Among all the new bazaar-like stalls, an old watch-repairer still had his shop, grey and barely noticeable among the crowds and colours. He wouldn't be around much longer, I thought – old Granada was pushing out the new. Or was it the other way around?

'Just like Morocco, eh?' Muhammad said as we parted, waving at the souk-like street. 'Tourists love it. It's great for the economy.'

I walked down to the Plaza Nueva in search of something stronger to drink, stepping over dog turds and dodging children clicking castanets as they rode their bicycles down the winding, stepped alleyways, no longer sure quite what I was looking for.

ALHAMBRA

Zine found me the day after my meeting with Muhammad. I was sitting in the Bib-Rambla square, the site of one of the old Arab gates to the city, watching a North African shoe-shiner convincing a tourist that his canvas walking sandals needed a good polish. Amazingly enough, the white-skinned camera-wielder had fallen for it and was happily raising his foot for the brush-and-cloth treatment, a handful of euros ready in his hand.

'You met a Spanish Muslim?' Zine said with a grin as he pinched my shoulder, sitting down in the empty chair beside me.

'Yes, Muhammad,' I said.

'He must have told you lots of interesting things about Islam and Spain,' he said, basking for a moment in his success at setting up the meeting.

'Yes, he did. Very interesting. How about you?' I asked. 'What've you been up to? I haven't seen you for days.'

'Oh, nothing.' He looked pleased with himself. That could only mean one thing.

'Have you been making peace with the Granada girls?' I asked.

'Only one!' he protested. 'Anyway, I've got a surprise for you.'

He pushed over a plastic envelope. Inside, decorated with bright, childlike colours, were two tickets for the Alhambra.

If you believed Camilo, the Alhambra palace, which sat like a sun-drenched cloud above the city and whose presence was so powerful it seemed to distort your internal compass, was just the product of a decadent, declining civilization. Christian Europe was about to enter its 'renaissance' and pull ahead of its southern Islamic rival when *al-qala al-hamra*, the Red Fort, was being built – a time when Moorish possession of the peninsula had been reduced to this small mountain kingdom in the south. While the history of the last years of Granada was a tale of labyrinthine in-fighting and corruption, a whole world away from the magnificence of the caliphal period some five hundred years earlier, to the north a new and expansive Spain was being born, a country on the point of discovering a new world and creating a mighty empire. In this context, the Alhambra was little more than an historical detail – beautiful, perhaps, a final starburst of a once-brilliant culture, but unimportant. Certainly not representative of Moorish Spain as a whole.

The Alhambra is much more than that, though, as most visitors will tell you. In fact for many, both Spanish and foreign, it symbolizes not only Al-Andalus but the very best of that period of the country's history; it is one of the greatest buildings in the whole of Europe as well as in the Islamic world. Without the Alhambra the Moors might never have existed in most people's imagination: like a fairy tale, it is, in Joseph Campbell's phrase, a primer for a certain picture-language of the soul. And it is one of the few places I have been to that can effect profound changes on people, even from a distance: my own interests in Spain and the Middle East had been sparked as a teenager by a chance discovery of some old photographs of the Alhambra – five idle minutes that later went on to change the course of my life. Something about its form, the elegance of its needle-like paired columns reflected in rippling pools of water, its ceilings of fine sculpture like snow, secret archways and infinite Arabesques, appealed to an uncommon force within me, as if I were discovering a new pulse beating to a slower, deeper rhythm.

'This place is timeless,' an elderly Englishman once explained to me as we both sat trance-like in the Patio of Myrtle.

The effect of the place was visible on people's faces: even a small boy, clutching his soldier-doll and grizzling, quietened as he stepped out into the brilliant light of the square, sliding his feet on the marble-slab floor as he raised his eyes to the incomprehensible geometrical squiggles on the capitals above. Others would momentarily break away from the confines of their guided tour to stop and stare and absorb something of the place. Who could resist wanting to capture a spark of this light and take it back home with them?

I had walked up the Cuesta de Gomérez at least a dozen times before on my way up to the Alhambra. Yet now, as before, the experience felt as new as if it were the first time. As we walked through the Pomegranate Gate, water gushed like a great sigh down cobbled gullies on either side of the road, while elms and horse chestnuts formed an arch of green above the path up the hill to the entrance. A sense of peace descended on us.

'*Al-hamra, Al-hamra*,' Zine began humming to himself as the gravel crunched beneath our feet. 'There's a song my mother used to sing about the Alhambra, but I can't remember the words. Old people used to sing it. How it used to be ours, and now the *faranj* – the Franks – have taken it.'

'Have you come to reconquer?' I asked.

'Oh,' he said with a smile, pretending the thought had never entered his mind, 'maybe.'

Powerful and beautiful, like so much to do with Moorish Spain, the Alhambra was also a bizarre mixture – a blend of styles and architecture from different ages, both Islamic and Christian. The fourteenth-century Nasrid palace, the most famous part of the castle complex, stood next to a fort built some three hundred years earlier, unremarkable save for its red colour and the views out over the city and the surrounding *vega*. Then there were the gardens of the Generalife stretching to a white summer palace further up on the hillside; the remains of the *medina*, the citadel, with the outlines of former streets and houses. And in the middle of it all a gigantic Renaissance bull-ring-like palace built by the Emperor Charles V. Heavy and squat, it sat as a permanent reminder of his grandparents' conquest of the city for Christendom; a statement of superiority at the heart of a once-proud civilization that said, 'This is ours.' Where the Nasrid palace was elegant and delicate, this was massive and hard, the walls built of gargantuan rocks, while the iron rings bolted on the outside looked better suited for tying up elephants than horses. It was said that in a different context it might have been an attractive building, but here the contrast with the subtleties of its neighbour meant it clashed inharmoniously.

Zine and I went straight into the Nasrid palace – with the millions of visitors passing through every year you were given a specific slot at which to arrive, and our allotted time was close to running out. The first room, the Mexuar audience hall, was full of tour groups peering up at the walls, where escutcheons of Charles V had been painted over the original Moorish walls. I pushed through and walked on to the outer courtyards, the gems of the place, leaving Zine to look around on his own.

Passing through a Z-shaped corridor, I stepped out into the blinding white of the Patio of Myrtle, the light of the sun reflected from all quarters and shining with a sea-like brilliance. I stopped a second to allow my eyes to adjust, but as before when crossing into this space, there was a sense of entering a different world. Not just the light: some subtler change seemed to take place as well.

Wa la ghalib illa Allah – No Conqueror but Allah. The Nasrid motto was repeated on the walls in sweeping Arabic script. The first Nasrid king, according to the legend, had been hailed as a hero when he returned from helping the Christian King Ferdinand III to take Seville in 1248: the price he had to pay for keeping Granada in Muslim hands. But Muhammad had protested when the people called him a conqueror. No, he said. There is no conqueror but God. And so the phrase had stuck. Ironic, perhaps, for a city best known for its eventual conquest by the Christians in 1492. Ferdinand and Isabel had worn Moorish clothes when they'd come to take possession of the palace.

I sat down on the ledge of a doorway in a corner of the patio, watching the dog-fighting martins reflected in the dark waters of the pool below. People filtered in slowly with a look of awe and puzzlement on their faces. Such was the quality of time, you felt you could watch the whole world passing through if you sat there long enough, like an ancient tree in a long-established garden, with each new generation of children climbing its branches to reach for its fruits.

It took me a moment to react when I saw Jasmin. Surely, I thought in my dream-like state, she was just one of several people I hadn't seen for years who would eventually come through the doorway if I remained in that same spot. She stood close to me, her trademark dyed-red hair just as it had been in Egypt, wearing big sunglasses and plenty of lipstick. Ten years, and she hadn't changed a bit.

'Jasmin?' I said, looking up at her.

We embraced. A former student of Arabic with me at Alexandria University, she was staying with friends on the coast and had come up to Granada for the day. But the Alhambra had already worked its effect on her, for she seemed as unsurprised as I was that we should meet here. Such things were only normal in the Nasrid palace. Either that, or she was still the laid-back German hippie she had been before.

Memories of when we had been in Egypt together flooded back. Strange that we should meet now as yet another Gulf War was getting under way. I remembered late-night parties at her flat, discussing the various 'nightmare scenarios' people had picked up during the course of the day. Would Saddam Hussein launch a chemical weapons attack? All-out Arab war might ensue. We could be on the threshold of Armageddon.

After a few glasses of Omar Khayyam wine, or Egyptian gin that tasted of bananas, things could start looking pretty bleak. At some point in the evening Judith, another German girl, would sit in the corner of the room and start muttering drunkenly about the end of the world, while Peter would put on a Bob Dylan record, light his hookah and tell everyone quietly to 'just relax'.

'Relax?!' Sara the Italian would screech. 'How relax when you can be hit any minute by a squid?'

'You mean Scud,' Peter would say.

'Squid. Scud. It doesn't matter.'

'Talk to your embassy if you're worried.'

'I can't. They've already evacuated.'

True to form, the Italian diplomatic corps had already retreated before a shot had been fired, leaving poor Sara on her own.

'We get married, then you will have Egyptian passport,' Ahmed would butt in. No one was quite sure where Sara had picked Ahmed up from, but he was a permanent feature at Jasmin's soirées, and plainly infatuated with Sara.

'You must help me. She is of white flesh. How can I win her heart?' he once whispered to me conspiratorially.

I never found the courage to tell him she had a fiancé waiting for her back in Genoa.

The build-up to a war is a strange period. Growing tension and fear, obsessive following of the news, a sense that the weight of the world is forcing itself upon your own life. Uncertainty about what horrors, if any, are to come. It is like a black form of flirtation. The flip side of the coin. Part of me had even been excited back then at the thought of war. Wasn't that why they existed in the first place? Because something in us sought to be pushed to the edge? It was a thrill. Deadly and horrific, but exciting.

This time, though, it felt different. Perhaps because I had changed, or the general mood had. But the build-up to this war was infused with a sense of dread.

We said our goodbyes and Jasmin walked on to see the rest of the palace.

Zine joined me shortly after, and together we passed from the Patio of Myrtle to the Patio of Lions. It was the most photographed piece of Al-Andalus, the Mount Fuji of Moorish Spain, with its intricate icicle-like *muqarnas* ceilings and the central fountain encircled by twelve stone lions, looking like beasts from a medieval manuscript expanded into three dimensions.

'This used to be the king's harem,' I told Zine with a grin.

He slapped me on the shoulder. 'Ha! Imagine all those girls!'

'I'm sure you can,' I said under my breath. From his low point in Almería, he seemed to be fully back on form.

'Who needs imagination anyway?' he said. He took a look around at some of the female tourists dotted among the columns. I was glad to see Jasmin had already gone. It would be too much if he tried to move in on her.

'This is a sacred place. For women only. They shouldn't let men in here,' he said with a mock frown. 'Except me. Of course.'

He began to move away, the look of a hunter searching for quarry shining in his black eyes.

'Make love, not war, Jasie. Wow, look at her.'

And he vanished into a crowd of Italian girls, their expensive leather rucksacks pulling white T-shirts tight across their young breasts.

Nasrid Granada had been a hedonistic place, the final gasp of a culture that had often been on the more liberal side within the Islamic world. Al-Andalus, at least until the invasions of fundamentalist Almoravids and Almohads, rarely shied away from worldly enjoyment, and was far from strict in adhering to Islamic prohibitions on alcohol, for example. The Moors even introduced certain wine grape varieties still used today, such as *verdejo* in the Rueda area of Castilla-León.

But Islam had never really had any ideas along the lines of 'original sin', and Granada in the fourteenth and fifteenth centuries, having freed itself from the austerity of the Berber Almohads and perhaps somehow aware that it was living the end of an era, hit the Epicurean accelerator big time.

'In Nasrid Granada the use, and abuse, of wine and hashish along with prostitution and sodomy extended to all levels of society,' one historian of Andalusi sexuality, Antonio Arjona Castro, had written. A culture that developed erection creams out of musk, mustard and the oil of lilies, or birds' brains mixed with jasmine, was one that clearly paid these matters much thought. Al-Andalus had, in fact, produced some of the greatest medical minds of the Middle Ages, and sexuality was an area of study they applied themselves to rigorously. Although some might have baulked at their prescription of elephant dung as a contraceptive.

The writings of these ancient medics were often illustrated with interesting case studies. Abd al-Rahman III's prime minister and physician, Yahya ibn Ishaq, had once had to cure a peasant with a swollen penis.

'Help me, O Minister, for I am about to die,' the poor man said, bursting into his surgery.

Ibn Ishaq saw that the man had a lump in his urethra. He called for a stone to be brought and placed it on the table, putting the man's penis on top. He then smashed his fist down, squashing the penis like a pancake. The peasant duly fainted, but shortly afterwards pus began flooding out, then urine.

'Go!' said Ibn Ishaq when the man woke up. 'You're cured.' The farmer thanked him. 'But don't go buggering your animals any more,' the doctor added. 'You got an oat from the beast's faeces stuck down your hole – that's what caused the lump and infection.'

The man confessed his guilt, then returned to his village.

Granada's greatest sexologist was a man called Ibn al-Khatib, doctor, historian, poet and, like Ibn Ishaq before him, a politician. A man ahead of his time, he stressed the benefits of sex for overall health, and the importance of female sexual enjoyment.

'A man must satisfy the needs of a woman more than his own,' he wrote in the 1300s, 'as it is common for women in this regard to be left with mere failure and disappointment, except, occasionally, by accident.'

Ibn al-Khatib also handed down details of the sex lives of some of the rulers and high officials of Granada, usually satirizing their homosexuality. He recorded one of the poems of the time:

O you who have made such fortune from your
  anus
You got wealth through one door and forgot to
  close it.
So much advantage did you wish to gain
You can't even push a finger through it now.

From Ibn al-Khatib's writing you got the impression
that sexual corruption in the Granadan court was rife.
The Sultan Ismail II was characterized as indolent and
effeminate, with a penchant for dressing in women's
clothes, and always happy to accept sexual favours in
lieu of debts owed to him.

Ultimately, Ibn al-Khatib himself fell victim to court
intrigues. In 1375 he was imprisoned after fleeing to
Morocco, and strangled to death on the orders of his
enemies. Yet his memory lived on in the Alhambra itself,
whose walls were decorated with verses from some of
his less bawdy poems.

I was victorious over the beauties in grace and
  crown,
Now the signs of Zodiac come down to me.

It was hard to quantify what the legacy to modern
Spain was, if any, of Moorish attitudes to sex. Sexual
relations between the two communities had been
commonplace: during the first centuries of Muslim
rule, intermarriage had been the norm, many of the
Arab and Berber arrivals settling down with local
women. Yet in the latter period of Al-Andalus, strict
laws had been drawn up in an attempt to prevent
intercourse between Moors and Christians, both sides
worried about their womenfolk being seduced by the

others: death by stoning was the usual punishment. There were even cases of Christian prostitutes refusing to sleep with Muslim clients. Nonetheless, there were plenty of tales of love affairs across the religious divide, many romanticized in popular literature – one of the most famous, the tale of Abencerraje and Jarifa, was published as late as 1565. Many Spaniards today still refer to their partner or lover as their 'half-orange', a legacy from the Moors, for whom an orange was a symbol of perfect love, the idea having been developed in Baghdad from Platonic concepts about sister-souls uniting to form a sphere.

Beyond that, the slang word for vagina, *chocho*, came from the Arabic *shusha*, but you didn't hear of politicians turning a blind eye to tax evasion, say, in exchange for a quick one. Corruption in high office, of which there was plenty, was usually of a financial nature. There was, though, a considerable lack of squeamishness about sex for such a Catholic country. Sex and sexuality were accepted as being natural, something to be enjoyed fully, even at ages younger than was commonly accepted in the rest of Europe – the age of consent here was thirteen. Pornography was everywhere, even on terrestrial TV channels, where at two o'clock in the morning you could easily find hard-core films with all kinds of variations on the usual theme. At the same time, however, there was little sense of living in a country of perverts. Physical contact was much closer than in any other European country I'd known. English friends of mine were shocked once to see a grandfather teasingly squeezing the sprouting breasts of his pubescent granddaughter on the beach. Here there was nothing 'dirty' about such behaviour – it was just playful fun, and a clear example of the reduced physical barriers between people.

Zine had vanished again. I carried on with the tour, past the Sala de los Abencerrajes. The shadowy room, decorated with fine icicles of *yeso* plasterwork, had been named after the slaughter of the Banu Sarraj clan that was said to have taken place there after one of their members was caught with the sultan's wife. Guides told you the red marks on the marble of the central fountain were the bloodstains from the massacre.

Finally I emerged into the gardens that stretched towards the Generalife further up the hill. It was a relief of sorts to get away from the crush of people, but although the rose bushes, cypress trees, interconnected pools of water and general lushness of the place continued the paradise-like effect from inside the palace, there was a sense of sadness that the experience had come to an end. It was at once sensual and other-worldly, unlike any other place I knew, and part of me was already longing to return.

I headed up and away into the maze of bushes and trees. Some areas were roped off but I slipped underneath, wanting to find a quiet corner somewhere just to sit for a moment, feel the sunlight filtering through the trees and let my mind wandor. Later I would find Zine and ask him what he thought about the place.

I came across him sooner than I'd expected. Pushing through some foliage in my quest for a hidden grove I heard hurried, excited voices and violent crunching of gravel underfoot. With a jolt I thought I'd been caught by some guards watching out for stray tourists, and quickly began inventing excuses to explain my 'crime'. But the girl who suddenly appeared from behind the trees simply ran off, fiddling with the buttons on her blouse. A second later Zine emerged, shirt open, his face flushed. He looked at me with horror. Then he swore, swinging his hand up and down in frustration.

'Jasie! Why didn't you say it was you?'

'What?'

'I thought we'd been caught,' he said.

'Who was that girl?'

'Eh? Oh, never mind. Shit, Jasie. Why didn't you say?' He began to smile, despite his anger.

'Zine, for Christ's sake. You weren't ... Were you?'

He laughed. 'I'm making peace between Muslims and Christians. I told you.'

'You can't have sex in the middle of the bloody Alhambra,' I said. 'What's got into you?' Despite my surprise, I couldn't help smiling along with him.

'She works here. Where else are we supposed to do it?'

'She *works* here?'

'Of course,' he said, tucking his shirt back into his trousers. 'How else do you think I got the tickets? I was just saying thank you.'

CÓRDOBA

'*E*gyptians,' Zine said as we followed in behind. 'Donkeys.'

Two Muslims walked ahead of us, their long black beards, white jellabas and knitted skullcaps oddly conspicuous, although they were standing outside what had once been the third-largest mosque in the world. Tourists glanced at them furtively, curious but frightened of offending.

Like Granada, Córdoba attracted visitors from all over the Islamic world: once the capital of Al-Andalus and the greatest city in western Europe, it was a memorial to a time when Muslims had been guardians of the most advanced culture in the world. The Moorish Golden Age had begun here when, during the tenth century, the Emir Abd al-Rahman III claimed the title 'caliph' for himself, in opposition to the established caliph in Baghdad and a rival contender in North Africa. The caliph was theoretically the religious head of the world Islamic community, in a similar way as the Pope is for Catholics. Home to five hundred thousand people – two hundred thousand more than today – Córdoba had boasted street lighting, five hundred mosques, three hundred public baths, fifty hospitals and seventy libraries – the Caliph Al-Hakam II (961–76) was said to have built one with half a million works in it. And it was filled with the advanced philosophical, scientific, mathematical, astronomical and medicinal learning that had been a part of the Islamic world since it came into contact with the disparate intellectual schools of Greece, Persia and India.

The giant hall of the Great Mosque was lit with low orange lamps, eight hundred and fifty delicate columns of marble and jasper suddenly branching out before us, line after line, like an exercise for drawing perspective gone mad. In the accumulative way of so much of Spain, the Moors had built sections of the mosque using materials from the Visigothic church that had previously stood on the site, itself partly made from the remains of an ancient Roman temple dedicated to the two-faced god Janus. And so Corinthian capitals on one side of an arch might be married with Pharaonic on the other, neither quite the right height, but with small adjustments made in every case to give the appearance of symmetry. Likewise the famous red and white striped horseshoe archways above our heads, which became such an architectural feature all over Spain that they turned into a kind of logo for Al-Andalus, were borrowed from earlier Gothic and Roman styles. Yet something about the combination was at once Moorish and unique.

Zine lagged behind, waiting for me to move further inside before breaking off to find his own way around. Arriving late in the city the night before, I'd finally persuaded him to stay at the *pensión* with me, arguing that even he would have trouble at that hour finding some available girl with a space in her bed. He knew I was right, but had been sulking ever since. In an earlier conversation I'd mentioned that *las cordobesas* were renowned as the prettiest girls in Andalusia, with their slim figures and long black hair tied back in shiny *malenas*; and it seemed he'd set his heart on discovering for himself the joys they offered.

'Wait till they taste the flesh of Zine,' he said. 'Then they'll wish the caliphs had never gone.'

This morning, though, the sour mood of the night before seemed to have intensified. He'd refused breakfast, instead locking himself in the bathroom for an hour, and when I spoke to him he pretended not to have heard. It annoyed me, but I assumed that once he'd seen the mosque he would cheer up a bit. And so I dragged him along, down the white twisting streets of the old Jewish quarter – the Judería – to the jewel of Andalusi religious architecture.

Once inside, he disappeared. A cluster of South American girls with tight-fitting jeans, all buttocks and chit-chat among the cloister-silence of the forest-like hall, tottered away towards the *mihrab*. Soon to become prey to Morocco's greatest love machine, I felt sure. I just hoped he succeeded with one of them, otherwise the rest of the day might become unbearable.

I wandered among the columns, trying to work out where one stage of the building of the mosque began and another ended. The ruler Abd al-Rahman I built the earliest section in the late eighth century, when the growing numbers of Muslims in the city meant that sharing the Visigothic church with the Christian population became impossible. Conversion to Islam among native Spaniards was slow during the first century or two of Al-Andalus, when the main incentive to switch faiths was merely financial – Christians and Jews were tolerated but had to pay a special tax. But in subsequent centuries the rate of conversion accelerated rapidly, so that by 1000, just a few years before Córdoba self-destructed in civil conflict, some 75 per cent of people were Arabic-speaking practising Muslims. Even when not converting to Islam, Spaniards adopted Muslim ways: the Christian Paul Alvarus, writing in Córdoba in the ninth century, had complained bitterly that young Christians in the city had forgotten their own language and culture.

'For every one who can write a letter in Latin to a friend,' he'd said, 'there are a thousand who can express themselves in Arabic with elegance, and write better poems in this language than the Arabs themselves.'

With the ever-growing numbers of Muslims, Córdoba's mosque had been added on to three times by Abd al-Rahman's successors, each maintaining the essential architectural style of the building, yet gradually extending it from a modest temple into a giant of a thing, like an ancient low-ceilinged warehouse. The original section was the most eclectic, and perhaps the most interesting, as the early Muslims plundered the Roman and Christian churches around them for building materials. Hence the anomalous yet harmonious mixture of ancient and Classical elements. As the extensions were added on, though, a uniformity crept into the architecture, so that the last section, built by the military dictator Al-Mansur in the late tenth century – the man who sacked Santiago de Compostela and kidnapped its cathedral bell – had an almost pre-fabricated feel to it. Until then, something of the mixture of artistic styles of the earliest mosque had been maintained: the highly decorated *mihrab* – the niche in the back wall that signalled the direction of prayer – had been a gift from the Byzantine emperor, and Christian Greek artisans had created the complex and colourful floral mosaic work.

Surprisingly, it was perfectly easy completely to ignore the massive cathedral the later Christian masters of the city had built inside the mosque. But once you noticed it, it was quite shocking, despite the syncretic nature of the building. Whereas previous additions had involved some degree of assimilation, Córdobans of the sixteenth century had simply plonked an overly decorated Baroque church right in the middle, like a boot in the face. It was little comfort that the word 'baroque' was of Arab origin, from *burga*, meaning uneven ground, reaching Europe through the word *barrocco* – a technical term used by Portuguese fishermen. The cathedral was simply brash and vulgar. Yet thankfully, perhaps because it was disguised from view by the host of columns, you could easily pretend it wasn't there.

I sat on a wooden bench in the far corner of the mosque, watching with slight edginess for signs of Zine while studying the building around me. Like many Friday mosques, this had been more than simply a prayer hall: it acted as a university, a meeting place, a community centre at the heart not only of the city but of Islamic Spain as a whole. Along these passage-ways would have walked all kinds of people, including, I fantasized, one of the most famous sons of Moorish Spain, Ibn Rushd.

Averroes, as he was known in the West, was one of those emblematic characters of the Middle Ages who stuck in your mind for the sheer presence he seemed to have and the lasting legacy of his genius over centuries, like a Moorish Chaucer, Dante or Albertus Magnus. Jorge Luis Borges had even written a short story about him, imagining his struggle to translate the terms 'tragedy' and 'comedy' into Arabic while reading Aristotle's *Poetics*.

Philosopher, astronomer, medic and jurist, Averroes lived during a period of cultural brilliance in Córdoba that coincided with the political decline of Moorish Spain. Internal conflicts had brought an end to the caliphate some hundred years before his birth, in 1031, and Al-Andalus split up into a patchwork of little kingdoms – some no bigger than a village and its surrounding area – often referred to as the 'Taifas'.

Christian forces in the north had taken advantage of the chaos to make deep inroads into Muslim-held territory, and in the face of their continued pressure, rulers in Al-Andalus called for help from a group of fundamentalist warrior monks in Morocco known as the Almoravids. The Almoravids duly crossed over and stopped the Christian advance. Instead of then returning to Marrakesh, however, they stayed and took over the remaining Moorish section of the peninsula. A few years later their place was taken by an even more hard-line bunch of Moroccans called the Almohads, rulers during Averroes' lifetime.

Reading about him in the gloom from a book I'd picked up that morning, I started to discover more. Born into a family of jurists, Averroes acted as physician and adviser to two of the Almohad rulers, was appointed religious judge or *qadi* (from which came the Spanish word for mayor, *alcalde*), while in his spare time he discovered sunspots and a new star.

He had also been a student of Ibn Tufayl, whose book *Hayy bin Yaqzan*, a story about a man growing up on a desert island, provided the inspiration for Defoe's *Robinson Crusoe* centuries later. Averroes' influence on Europe, however, was more immediate. He provided a comprehensible study of Aristotle's work that was quickly translated into Latin for Christian scholars struggling to get to grips with the body of Greek philosophy. Western thinkers later dubbed him simply 'the Commentator' in recognition of his role, and St Thomas Aquinas admitted that much of his own inspiration in resolving the supposed conflict between Christian revelation and reason had come from the Spanish Muslim. Such was the respect for him in Europe that Dante had even given him a place in Limbo next to Aristotle himself. His works were standard textbooks in Western universities until the sixteenth century (in Mexico until the 1830s).

There was more to Averroes than a beginner's guide to Aristotle, though. The author of over eighty books, he expounded ideas on the collective unconscious eight hundred years before Jung, insisted on the importance of a good digestion and sound bowel movements for general health, and once famously issued a fatwa saying that Muslims living in Christian-controlled lands should emigrate to Muslim-held territory: 'The obligation to emigrate from the lands of unbelief will continue till the day of judgement.'

His popularity with the fanatical rulers of the day had not lasted, though. There was a story of how, on being accused of heresy and supposedly insulting the Almohad leader, he'd been ordered to stand at the entrance of the mosque, to be spat at by all 'true believers' walking by. Fallen from grace, he was sent into exile, and eventually died in Marrakesh, far from his beloved Córdoba; 'God's greatest city', he had called it. The modern city reciprocated the compliment after a fashion by naming a street in his honour.

Almohad control of Al-Andalus came to an end shortly after Averroes' death with another big push by Christian forces southwards. The Moors were defeated at the battle of Navas de Tolosa in 1212, and in the subsequent forty-odd years almost the entire peninsula was taken over by the Christians – Valencia, Córdoba and Seville were all conquered in this period. Only one area – the Kingdom of Granada – held out. It continued to do so for the next two and a half centuries.

I found Zine in the Orange Tree Court that served as a sort of ante-chamber to the indoor section of the mosque. Tourists sat on low walls in the shade of the trees, writing postcards, changing the film in their cameras, or, as one German was doing with a certain irreligious devotion, simply picking his nose while his girlfriend spoke to a friend back home on her mobile phone.

Zine, I saw as I walked towards him, was just finishing talking to the Egyptians we'd seen entering earlier on. He seemed friendly with them, his manner at odds with his previous hostile reaction. Now he looked almost deferential. I smiled as I walked towards him: at least now he might have got over the black mood of that morning. With any luck I might be able to drag him along that afternoon to the Medina Azahara ruins outside the city.

'This place is dirty,' he said as I approached him. 'I'm leaving.' His face, just a few seconds before all smiles with the Egyptians, had dropped into a deep scowl. 'Look at all these people. This is a mosque!'

I was surprised by the sudden anger in his voice.

'They don't even take off their shoes. Why can't they treat it with more respect?'

I didn't take this outburst seriously. He hadn't taken his shoes off either.

'I thought you were more interested in the girls inside than the mosque itself,' I said.

'I don't walk into a church shouting *Allahu akbar* – Allah is great,' he said, ignoring me. 'They treat Islam like shit. In Morocco we keep tourists out of the mosques.'

He turned his face to one side, trying to control his rage, a strand of curly black hair falling into his eyes. He flicked it out angrily with his finger. I could see that he might find the tourists annoying, but it was still not a reaction I would have expected from him.

'This is *not* how it should be,' he said.

And for a second I saw clearly how many gaps there were between us, even though we had been slowly and sometimes tetchily getting to know one another better as we travelled along. The Egyptians appeared to have hit some hidden puritanical nerve in him. Friendly leg-pulling now would almost certainly not be a good idea.

'Stay among the dirt, *la suciedad*, if you want.' And he turned to walk back through the pointed archway of the main entrance into the streets of the Jewish quarter, muttering in Arabic to himself.

Totally confused, I walked after him, keeping my distance in case he blew up in my face. God knows what had really got into him. Normally I might simply have let him walk off – he had an unnatural knack of finding me whenever he needed to, and perhaps in a few hours or days he might have cooled off. But I wasn't planning on staying in Córdoba long: we'd already been several days in Granada. I was beginning to want to get him to Niebla finally and leave him there.

A waiter at one of the pavement cafés brought things unexpectedly to a head. Stepping in front of Zine just as he was trying to get past, he blocked his way, making him stop abruptly on the ancient street made narrower by the tourist shops bursting out of their doors and windows on either side. For a moment I had got too close, so as Zine stopped I walked straight into the back of him, scraping his heel with my shoes.

It may have simply been a reaction to the sudden pain, or perhaps it gave him the excuse he'd wanted, but with a jolt I felt his forearm swing round and crash into my neck, just below the jawline. There was a loud clicking sound inside my head as a number of vertebrae seemed to rub against one another, and with a shock I stumbled backwards, almost falling over the people crushing behind us in the pre-lunch rush.

'*Oye, tío. Joder. ¿Lo has visto?* Fuck. Did you see that?'

A woman sitting at the café gave a yelp, and I quickly became aware of the curious attention we were receiving. I struggled to stand up straight, rubbing my numbed face and apologizing to the people I'd bumped into. Looking up, I saw that the waiter was eyeing Zine, as though trying to decide whether to beat him up himself or let the police do the job.

'*Perdón, perdón,*' I shouted. People were beginning to gather round us, and from the look on their faces it was clear who they'd decided was guilty. Zine was automatically viewed with suspicion: you couldn't bury centuries of burning heretics at the stake that easily.

'It's my fault,' I said hastily, raising my voice above the din. 'I tripped and bumped into my friend here.' I put my hand on Zine's shoulder. 'I must have pushed him forwards.'

The waiter looked at me with disdain. To be Moroccan was low down in his estimation, but to be a foreigner from the north was clearly little better. Still, you didn't kick tourists out of the country just for tripping up in the street. He tipped his head to the side and clicked his tongue, then turned back to serving tables as though we weren't there: he'd understood, but wanted to demonstrate that his pride had been wounded at the same time. Some of the men standing around were still looking at Zine aggressively, though. One of them spat on the ground. It seemed a good idea to move on.

'*A ver si tiene documentación.* I wonder if he's got any paperwork,' I could hear one say.

I grabbed Zine's arm and we pushed through the crowd. More people were peering over to see what was going on. You could tell the English tourists because they were the only ones not stopping to look.

We headed down narrow alleyways, past windows shaped like miniature Moorish archways, and flashes of green as the heavy foliage of proud patio gardens came into view through open doorways: brief glimpses of paradise. Zine's body was stiff and tense, his muscles barely giving way as I continued to grip his arm, half pushing him along as I tried to find our way out of the old city and away from the crowds. He said nothing, his teeth clenching together, creating an ugly skull-like effect in his face.

What, I thought to myself, was I doing with this man? I should take him to the station, put him on a bus for Niebla and let him sort himself out. I was buggered if I was going to carry on like this. But despite his mood swings and hitting me in the face, the bastard, I actually enjoyed his company and the sharpness he brought to this journey. He'd become an essential part of my search for Moorish Spain.

Ten minutes later, we sat down at a bar just outside the city walls, a statue of Averroes looking down paternally at us while American girls tried to straddle his knees to have their photo taken. Crows peppered the midday sky, flying in over the coffee-coloured Guadalquivir with its ruined Moorish waterwheels.

In the street behind us a religious procession passed, all brass band and hand-clapping as men in brown cloaks took it in turns to carry an enormous float with life-size statues depicting the scene of Judas's betrayal of Jesus. The men rocked the float from side to side, or backwards and forwards, rhythmically to the music, as in a heavy primitive dance. Then more clapping came and the bearers would appear sweating from underneath, and change places with their mates. The party atmosphere seemed at odds with the tragic scene represented above their heads.

Three Córdoban girls pulled away from the procession and walked past us, their long black hair, dark skin and low-cut blouses giving an Oriental pride to their beauty, and a deep, animal awareness of the power they had to attract. You could see it in their gait and posture; they were like elegant Nubians with their shopping towering up from their heads, conscious of being the most alluring creatures on earth.

Zine looked straight ahead, unseeing, eyes pale.

'There is sickness here,' he said.

SEVILLE

'*Y*ou sure your friend's OK? He's been gone a while.'

I turned my head away from the stage and looked back through the cigarette and hashish smoke in the direction of the toilets to which Zine had disappeared earlier. Glancing up at a clock on the wall I reckoned he must have been gone about fifteen minutes.

'He'll be all right. Probably got food poisoning or something.'

Amadeo laughed. 'It's usually us who get gut rot when we go to his country, not the other way round. Perhaps he can't stomach all the ham.'

I poured out more thick red wine into our scratched tumblers. I was worried about Zine. We had got over the worst of our fight in Córdoba, without actually having managed to apologize to one another, but he was still less talkative than normal and had spent the last couple of days moping around, barely lifting himself out of bed. This time, at least, he hadn't protested when I insisted he shared a room with me. I still wasn't sure what was wrong, but was convinced he was in no fit state to go cruising the streets of Seville looking for a 'bed' for the night. It might just be fatigue,

I thought, or perhaps some stomach bug, judging from the amount of time he'd been spending in bathrooms. If he didn't show signs of improvement soon I might have to get him some medication.

He had insisted on coming with me to the flamenco *tablao* that night: having seen him look so rough all day, I thought perhaps he was feeling better and felt like seeing something of the city – Ishbiliya, the Moors had called it, and Zine still referred to it by the old Arabic name. On the way we had passed the Giralda, brightly lit above the orange trees and droppings from horses ferrying tourists in shiny black carriages. The bell tower and symbol of the city was the Almohads' greatest architectural legacy in Spain – the minaret to the mosque that had previously stood where now the Christian temple took its place – sister minarets in similar style still stood in Marrakesh and Rabat. Thick and square, with geometric patterns in brickwork creeping up its sides, the Christian King Alfonso X 'the Wise', when still a prince conquering the city for his father Ferdinand III, had saved the tower from destruction by Muslims fearful of it falling into Christian hands.

Across the square stood the Alcázar: Seville's Alhambra – a lusciously decorated Moorish palace still used as a royal residence when the king came down from Madrid. Its delicate archways, pools of water and *yeso* plastered ceilings, however, had been built for a Christian king – Pedro the Cruel; this defender of the Catholic faith had the royal escutcheon painted on the walls of his bedchamber emblazoned with Arabic script proclaiming, 'Glory to our Sultan Don Pedro, may Allah aid and protect him.'

Zine had been fine for the first hour at the *tablao*,

pushing his way towards the front to grab us a seat just under the little wooden stage. Then Amadeo had shown up, an old flamenco friend of mine I hadn't seen for years – he was spending the weekend in Seville before heading back up to Madrid in the morning. The three of us managed to take over one end of the refectory tables that stretched the length of the hall, trying to ignore the hollering of some French language students behind us. Carboneras was a place to talk and drink while listening to the live performances in front, but the noise that night meant sometimes you could barely hear anything that was being played.

Amadeo and I quickly caught up on each other's news. He'd been on the fringes of a group of *flamencos* I'd known in the capital, but we'd never really got to know one another as much as I'd have liked. This would be a great opportunity. I knew he was interested in the history of flamenco and Spanish folk music. 'Talking to Amadeo's like talking to a book,' they'd said of him. Who better to explain the Moorish influence on it all?

Seville had been the musical centre of Spain for some thousand years. Court music had flourished in Córdoba, the caliphal capital, but when this started mixing with popular styles and new forms of music started being developed, Seville quickly took over as the musical centre of gravity.

'When a wise man dies in Seville,' Averroes said, 'they take his books to be sold in Córdoba. And when a musician dies in Córdoba they take his instruments to be sold in Seville.'

This proud, floral city, with its perfume of orange blossom and its bright, violent colours, seemed to live off music. A whole folk dance – Sevillanas – had been named after it, and you could barely hear a flamenco song without some reference to the Triana district on the east bank of the Guadalquivir.

> *El río Guadalquivir se quejaba una mañana:*
> *Me tengo que elegir entre Sevilla y Triana,*
> *Y yo no sé dónde acudir.*

> The River Guadalquivir sighed one morning:
> I have to choose between Seville and Triana,
> And I don't know which way to go.

For centuries Triana, a run-down area, like a dirty reflection of the imperial city on the opposite bank, had been home to Gypsies and workers, whose lasting legacy came from their music and dancing. It was not a romantic place: in fact some guidebooks warned you not to go there, or if you did, at least to keep a tight grip on your handbag. A few bars on the riverbank were cashing in on its reputation as one of the mother-districts of flamenco, but for the most part it was just a fairly ordinary place with little charm, and rather a disappointment after all the lyrics I'd heard sung about it over the years. Apart from a dance school in someone's front room and a couple of shops selling bright red and yellow Sevillana dresses, with their long and rather kitsch frilly tails, there was little to show this was a flamenco heartland. Crossing back over the muddy river to the city centre in a freak rain shower, I had felt disappointed at not being able to perceive its supposed magic.

Even though I'd been involved in flamenco for years, I had never got to grips with the part the Moors

173

had had to play in it. I knew about the theories that the word flamenco itself came from the Arabic *felah manju*, or escaped peasant, and that *ole*, that most Spanish of words, was in fact a borrowing from the Arabic phrase *wallah*, or 'By God!', as I'd already tried telling Salud. But apart from that, I still wasn't clear what the influence of the Moors on flamenco had actually been.

'No one's clear about it. That's the problem,' Amadeo shouted in my ear above the din of Carboneras when I brought the subject up. 'Flamenco's an oral art form first of all, so there aren't many written records to give us clues. Then it's a mixture of Gypsy stuff, Andalusian folk music and some Moorish stuff as well. It's almost impossible to separate all the different strands. *¿Me explico?* You see what I mean?'

Amadeo was the best kind of *flamenco* to my mind: a Bohemian who had seen some of the harsher sides of life, and had probably been led into darker parts of himself through the music. But he had come out on the other side with a deep love of life and a calm awareness that every day might be his last. His heavily lined face, the dark rings under his eyes and his volcanic voice were the kind of traits I'd come across often among middle-aged Spanish musicians, but behind it all there was something of a light that shone, like the appearance of someone who had not only lived, but learnt something too. I knew that for years he'd kept himself alive busking around Europe, on the Underground or in the street, with the odd gig here and there at a bar or pub: a kind of flamenco troubadour, picking up bits and pieces of musical knowledge as he wandered the world. His style of playing was a bit old-fashioned for some, but his sense of rhythm, they always said, was perfect.

'Islamic music has styles, a bit like the different *palos* in flamenco,' he went on. 'They call them *maqams*, each one with its own distinctive key and beat. You know, like *bulerías* or *alegrías* for us. I've heard Mauritanian musicians playing the same rhythms as a *petenera*.'

We both touched the wooden bench beneath us to ward off the evil eye as he mentioned the secret *palo*. Similar in structure to a *soleá* or a *bulería* – yet with one important difference – the *petenera* was thought by Gypsies to have some magical power about it, so that for years no one recorded it or taught it outside a select group. Even mentioning its name, as now, brought out the superstitious in most people.

'I think maybe that's why we think of it as the "mother *palo*",' Amadeo said, straightening himself to let a couple of young girls squeeze past behind us and then waiting till they had moved on before continuing. 'Any twelve-beat flamenco rhythm finds its origins in it, and it probably comes from Africa or the Middle East, but no one is allowed to talk about it. You see what I mean? It's taboo.'

I nodded. Across from our table a group of Gypsies were sitting at the edge of the stage, a young man with typically long hair hunched over his cigarette whom I took to be a singer, and next to him a man of about fifty or more, dressed in a grey suit, with white shirt and crimson cravat, and grey boots of soft thin leather, a gold chain hanging loosely from his wrist, his hand resting on an ebony cane. Proud and composed, he looked at me for a minute as though there were some connection between us and smiled like a cat before

175

turning to speak to his companion. It was a rare occurrence among Gypsies – more often than not they barely acknowledged your existence. But every now and again – it had happened to me perhaps two or three times before – some of them opened up and seemed to communicate on some non-verbal level.

'What about the Gypsy influence, then?' I asked, turning back to Amadeo.

'This is exactly what I mean about the *petenera*,' he said. We both touched wood again. It felt vaguely blasphemous mentioning the word twice in quick succession, especially as we were in one of the biggest flamenco *tablaos* in Seville, surrounded by hundreds of aficionados. I wasn't sure if we shouldn't get up and carry on the conversation in some private dark corner of the narrow Moorish alleyways outside, but then I remembered Zine. We would have to stay till he got back. I looked towards the toilets again: still no sign. Perhaps he was trying to chat someone up at the bar. Somehow I doubted it, though.

'The Gypsies were responsible for the change in the *palo*,' Amadeo said. 'The shift of the first beat from the "one" back to the "twelve". That's how we get *soleares* and other *palos* from it. That's their genius. Simple, but it changes the entire *feeling* of the music.'

'OK,' I said, trying to get back to our original theme, 'apart from, er, that *palo*, are there any other obvious Moorish influences in flamenco?'

'In Yemen I often heard *tanguillos*,' he said. And with his tongue he began clicking the gallop-like rhythm of the flamenco song, marking the beat with his finger like a conductor. 'Then there's our instruments.' He began to list them, ticking each item off on the fingers of his right hand, each nail a perfectly filed claw

176

hardened and protected for playing with superglue. 'Drums, trumpets, hornpipes and rebecs, the precursor of the viol family, all come from the Middle East. Tambourine? *Pandereta* comes from the Arabic *bandair*. The guitar? Comes from the Arabic lute. Can't have flamenco without the guitar. And that's largely Ziryab's influence. See what I mean?'

Ziryab had long fascinated me. A man who was reported to have brought toothpaste and chess to Europe in the ninth century, he was a musician of exceptional ability. His jealous teacher had had him banished from the imperial court in Baghdad when the young apprentice revealed the full extent of his talents at a concert before the caliph. Soon afterwards Ziryab ended up in Spain, a distant and politically independent outpost of the Muslim world, till then effectively cut off from the cultural flowering that was taking place in the Islamic heartlands. Settling in Córdoba as the emir's court musician, he introduced the backwater Andalusis to the latest fashions from what was then the Paris or New York of its day: seasonal colours for clothes (dark in winter, white in summer); short haircuts for both men and women – veils and turbans didn't become the norm until much later on; table etiquette; home furnishings; and of course, the latest tastes in music. This Beau Brummell of Al-Andalus, as he has often been described, also revolutionized the lute, effecting a major step into its development into the guitar by adding a fifth string. The original four had represented the classical humours; what was missing, according to Ziryab, was the 'heart'. Over a thousand years later, the flamenco guitarist Paco de Lucía named one of his records after this

177

ancient style guru in recognition of the debt flamenco owed him.

Apart from this one extraordinary man, though, there were plenty of other echoes from the Arab world in Spanish music. A flamenco equivalent of the lyric filler 'yeah, yeah, yeah' was *lolailo* or *lelele*. Might it have come from the Muslim proclamation of faith *La illaha illa-llah*? The meaning had been lost, but the words sounded almost exactly the same. You could easily imagine some medieval Christian or Gypsy hearing Muslims chanting this phrase, then copying it, much as Europeans with no interest or knowledge of baseball today walk around wearing Yankee caps.

Then there were the *saetas*.

'Ah, now that really is an Arabic thing, *pues*,' Amadeo said when I mentioned them.

Seville was one of the capitals of *saetas* – haunting chants sung in honour of the Virgin or Jesus during the parades of Easter Week, their strange, twisting melodies with sliding quarter-tones sounding almost exactly like muezzin calls to prayer.

> *Y las golondrinas quitaron*
> *las espinas a Jesús*
> *y no pudieron desclavarlo*
> *con sus picos de la cruz.*

> The swallows picked
> The needles from Jesus's hair,
> But with their beaks were unable
> To bring him down from the cross.

Often you'd hear a reference to 'those Jewish traitors' thrown in just for good measure, as waves of melancholy and woe were whipped up into a kind of therapeutic mass public release of grief. A bit like the annual Shi'ite Ashura festivals in Iran and Iraq. Shi'ism, an early break-away branch of Islam, had never got much of a foothold in Al-Andalus, which remained decidedly orthodox, or Sunni, throughout its history. Yet the similarities between Holy Week and Ashura were striking: the death of a holy man – Imam Hussein, in the case of the Shi'ites – was marked by massive processions and public displays of weeping and self-flagellation. Another Muslim echo in the Spanish Easter festivities was the organization of the participants into brotherhoods, or *hermandades*. These cloaked figures with pointed hoods that masked their faces had been the inspiration for the get-up of the Ku Klux Klan, but originated in semi-secret religious societies in Al-Andalus: they still existed in Morocco today, taking part in processions of worship on feast days to local holy sites.

'*Saetas*,' Amadeo shouted in my ear as I strained to hear him above the sound of the new flamenco *cantaor* starting his set, 'comes from the Arabic word *ghaita*. They used to sing them in the evenings to entertain the kings and caliphs. You can still hear them sung in some parts of Algeria. And they still call them *ghaitas*.'

I smiled as I turned back to look at the performance on stage. The singer was slumped in his chair, and had adopted the usual round-shouldered posture to achieve the right resonance in the thorax. His hair glistened under the spotlights from the wet-look gel he'd smeared onto his scalp before coming on. I loved these little nuggets of information about Spain, these anomalies, where the Christian and Muslim elements of the country quietly and secretly interlocked and welded together. The whole thing might have been labelled Catholic today, but there was no doubting the Moorishness both of flamenco and of the Easter Week celebrations. The legacy was there if you looked for it; all it took was to peel away some of the disguise. Rocks, gems: one of Musa's jewels to observe and admire.

'The Church, of course, knew about all this Moorish and Gypsy influence on music. That's why they banned certain scales. The flamenco scale – the one we use, right? – that was banned by the Inquisition. They said it was the work of the Devil. Ha! Just because we jump three semitones. *¿Me explico?* Can't do that, they said.'

He gave me a look that suggested such restrictions were never very far from being reinstated, as though the authorities were always on the lookout for ways to impose more limitations on us.

'I went to Valladolid about ten years ago when they were having their annual fiesta,' he said. '*Matajudios*, they called it. A festival celebrating some ancient massacre of the Jews. Can you believe it? Some things take a long time to change.'

Perhaps a few months earlier I would have been more shocked at this, but now it seemed to fit in well to the complex picture of absorption and rejection I was piecing together.

A quick glance at Amadeo's watch brought me swiftly back to the present: half an hour, perhaps more, had passed since Zine had headed off to the toilet. Too long for just an ordinary case of the runs. He'd hardly drunk anything either. I wavered for a moment between going off to investigate and giving

him a few more minutes. If he was still in the
bathroom he was bound to be in the kind of state
where no one – least of all me at the moment – would
be welcome. Lifting my head up above the late-night
crowd, I tried once again to see if I could spot him at
the bar or in some other part of the *tablao*, but there
was no sign of him.

'Excuse me a moment,' I said to Amadeo as I
uncurled myself from the bench.

The toilets were in a corner of the hall, near the
entrance to the garden section of the *tablao*. They said
that even the great Camarón had performed here on
occasion, which was probably why so many foreigners
had homed in on the place. It was low season –
autumn – yet the blond heads of several dozen
Scandinavians and Northern Europeans punctuated
the residually black and dark-brown patina all around
us. Just outside the doorway a group of five American
boys in their early twenties, pumped with
Hemingway-esque bravado and sangría, were
challenging one another to fist fights, their cat-calling
managing to rise above the Spanish din of several
hundred voices all talking at once.

'I could take you on right here and now, pal.'

'You're full of shit, Todd.'

You had to take your hat off to the Spanish at
moments like these: rather than creeping away or
stiffening in awkward English silence, they merely
talked and laughed that bit louder, effectively blotting
out the socially undesirable with their own noise.

'Zine?' I called at the one locked cubicle. The floor
was covered in a grey-brown coating of well-trodden
piss, cigarette butts making clean-sweeping streaks
where people had slipped on them as they passed

181

in and out. There was no response. I looked around to see if there was anyone who might have noticed something wrong. Two men stood with their backs to me at the urinals, concentrating on other matters in hand.

'Zine!' I knocked this time. 'Anyone there?'

'Looks like you might have a wait on your hands,' one of the men said, zipping up his fly as he stepped past me back into the hall. I smiled, but a lump was starting to develop in my throat. If Zine was in there, perhaps I'd seriously underestimated how ill he was. Still smarting from Córdoba, I hadn't been too keen to ask questions, hoping things would sort themselves out, my mind fixed on our eventual arrival in Niebla and the day when I could finally deliver on my promise and get him a job – and off my hands. But what if he'd fallen unconscious? With an inward groan I could see myself having to break down the door. Perhaps I could get the American kids to give me a hand. But it wasn't easy breaking down doors without people noticing. I'd have to get the management involved, which meant ambulances, the police, paperwork – and the next boat back to Morocco.

'Zine!' I shouted this time, a note of desperation in my voice. There was a kick on the door from the inside.

'Is that you, Zine?' I said. A sign of life at least. 'Zine?' There was always the chance, of course, I was just annoying the hell out of some complete stranger quietly trying to have a late-night crap.

'Jasie,' came the weak reply, with a note of self-pity. But before I could say anything else the latch had been pulled back and a white-faced Zine had pulled me

182

inside the cubicle with him, locking the door again as I tried to avoid getting too close to the well-used lavatory.

'What's going on?' I said as he turned round again to face me. 'Are you ill? You've been in here for ages.' From the force with which he'd grabbed my shirt front, I sensed this was not as life-threateningly serious as I'd been starting to imagine.

'Jasie . . .' The skin around his eyes was swollen, there was a certain pallor around his cheeks, and a distinct wobble was developing in his chin.

'What's the matter, Zine?' I put my hand on his shoulder to try to calm him down.

He looked at me, leaning his head towards mine with the expression of someone faced with a certain and violent death. 'It's red, Jasie. ¡Hmar!' he screamed, a flood of moistened breath issuing from his mouth, and pointed down at the toilet bowl. After a moment's hesitation, partly out of concern that my Moroccan companion had finally lost it, partly for fear of what I was about to set my eyes on, I turned and looked. The usual stains and griminess of a public convenience were there, as I had expected, but I was surprised to find that in addition there was a pinky hue to the water at the bottom.

'Blood!' Zine screamed again, and placed his head against my arm with a dramatic sob, his left hand placed over his groin in a protective gesture. 'I'm going to die!'

I looked down again at the water in the bowl. The moment that every man secretly fears – when he sees the most treasured part of his anatomy spurt forth the wrong colour liquid – had just come for Zine. Yellow? Fine. White? Even better, at least in the right circumstances. But red? Ooh, that was a nasty one, tapping into primeval fears of blood, death and having your knob chopped off. And, rightly enough, Zine felt that his entire life had come to a sudden and horrific end.

'Jasie, help me!' His knees giving way, he hung on to me as though he was being dragged down into the icy pit of Hell itself.

'Come with me,' I said, pushing my arm under his shoulder to support his weight and slipping the catch on the door.

'No!' he screamed again. 'Just let me die here.'

Ignoring his protests, I managed to get him out of the cubicle and back into the hall, his head bobbing up and down as though he'd just taken a bullet through the carotid artery. I half expected stretcher-bearers with little red crosses painted on their helmets to come rushing over and take him away to the nearest field hospital, but no one paid us any attention. A group of people who looked like managers of the place were busy ushering the American youths away, their patience finally tested by their boisterous sabre-rattling, so I slipped over to their empty seats and sat Zine down.

'Wait here,' I said, trying to keep him from sliding to the floor. He gave me a half-conscious grunt of acknowledgement, quickly falling back into the role of dying victim.

'Amadeo,' I said, getting back to my seat, 'you don't know any clap clinics in Seville, do you?'

It was nine o'clock in the morning when we got to the centre on the Calle Baños. The place didn't open till ten, but Zine wanted to be the first in line, convinced his only chance of cheating certain death would be to get whatever pills they gave him down his throat as fast as possible.

We arrived as the ghost-light of early morning was giving way to a muggy warmth that barely seemed to leave the city, no matter what time of year you came. July and August were the worst, when the temperature stayed at a steady forty plus. But even in winter you often saw girls in sleeveless dresses. The cooler months of the year were really the best times in places this far south: to compare someone to 'a summer's day' was bordering on insult.

Despite our early arrival, a handful of girls, mostly black, were already hanging around outside the locked clinic doors. Their long, shapeless legs protruded from tiny leopard-skin skirts of varying shades – pink, brown, orange – and they leant against the wall with tired bodies. Each girl had her little handbag tucked under her elbow, and their eyes were half closed after being up all night. Astonishingly young, most of them; they looked barely fifteen or sixteen.

'You'll be all right there,' Amadeo had said. 'They're used to dealing with *putas* so it's all anonymous. No difficult questions.'

I hadn't really expected him to have a clue about where Zine and I should go, merely asking him on the off-chance and as a way of filling him in on what had happened. But he'd given us the address straight away, as though, apart from being a flamenco guitarist, he also worked in his spare time as a counsellor for people with STDs.

'Old girlfriend of mine used to work there,' he said. Seemed plausible enough, and I wasn't intending to ask anything more when he added that he met her there when he went for a check-up himself 'after a mild touch of gonorrhoea'.

'Right,' I said, not really wanting to know this. 'What was her name? Do you want me to say "hi"?'

'Mati. She doesn't work there any more.'

Good, I thought. Having a person on the inside of an organization usually helped smooth out most procedures in Spain, but in this case I was quite happy for there not to be any more personal contact than the bare minimum.

Zine sat on the pavement, his head in his hands, moaning to himself in Arabic. He rocked from side to side like a child soothing himself. We'd only slept for a couple of hours back at the *pensión* before heading out again, Zine writhing like a madman on the bed while he kept one protecting hand over his crotch, refusing to undress or wash or, heaven forbid, go to the toilet again. I hoped that with the sweat and dehydration he wouldn't have to piss, but several hours had passed now since I'd dragged him out of the *tablao* and I hated to think what kind of pressure his bladder might be under.

'Don't worry too much about him,' Amadeo had said as we left Carboneras. 'It's nothing. Just shock. They'll just give him some antibiotics, it'll burn when he pisses for a while, but he'll be right as rain in a few days. It's who he got it from and who he's given it to that you've got to worry about.'

And it was this more than anything else that had been passing through my mind all morning. It might have been useful to find out from Amadeo how he had dealt with the situation back when he met Mati, but he would already be halfway to Madrid by now, having caught the seven-thirty Ave train. I thought back to the girls Zine had slept with since we'd been on the road – or at least the ones I was aware of. Was there any way we could get in touch with them? Or would it even be necessary? I wasn't sure how long the incubation period for gonorrhoea was. Would Lucía be at risk?

At five past ten, the doors to the clinic finally opened. From his slumped position on the floor, Zine leapt up and pushed his way to the front, ahead of the prostitutes, and spoke nervously and rapidly to the woman letting them in.

'Concha at the desk there will take your details,' she said, stifling a morning yawn and pointing behind her, a lifetime of dealing with genital warts and HIV making her blasé about just another simple case of the clap.

I stood out in the corridor reading the sexual-health notices pinned on the walls as they dealt with Zine in one of the consulting rooms: 'ITCHING?'. Most of the prostitutes seemed like regulars and were dealt with speedily by the people on duty, picking up condoms or what looked in some cases like bags of prescription drugs. A couple, though, had stayed on, their heads lurching forward as they drifted off to sleep then woke with a start to exchange brief words with each other. For a moment I thought I caught some English, but wasn't sure. Many of the girls had what looked like ritual scars running down their cheeks, like thick strokes of a brush dipped in deep-purple paint.

'Did you want to speak with someone?' the girl at the desk asked.

'No, thanks. I'm here with a friend,' I said, and laughed as I found myself using the clichéd line.

'Tell me,' I said, taking a step closer, 'how serious is gonorrhoea?'

Ten minutes later, Zine stepped out with a bunch of leaflets, a look of utter seriousness on his face which told me immediately that the worst had failed to happen and the crisis was now at an end. The health worker had told me that the first symptoms usually developed two to five days after contact, which at least meant that Lucía was almost certainly all right, and had confirmed Amadeo's assurance that it could be dealt with by a single dose of antibiotics.

He'd probably caught it from the girl in Granada. The only problem now would be seeing how he dealt with having lost face so dramatically the night before. He walked past me with a grunt and headed for the door.

'*Disculpe*,' said a woman's voice behind me. I turned and then called to Zine.

'No,' said the doctor – a small woman with thin dark eyes and tightly knit curly hair. Better suited to a police uniform than a white coat, I thought. 'I want to talk to you.'

I stopped. God forbid that she was going to ask for papers. What with the new law on foreigners, things had tightened up. Maybe they did want to take down our details. But then why had she called to speak to *me*? I took a hesitant step towards her.

'*Mamada* – Blowjob,' she said curtly when I'd got closer.

I did a double take.

'*Mamada*,' she said again. 'You understand Spanish, don't you?'

'Yes, all too well.'

'I need you to give me the English translation. I take it you're English, or American?'

I nodded.

188

'It's these Nigerian sex workers,' she said, indicating over my shoulder at the prostitutes in the corridor. 'They don't speak any Spanish and we're trying to educate them about high-risk sex activities, but of course all our English is medical, from the textbooks. They don't understand me when I say "fellatio".'

'No, of course. I quite understand,' I said.

'Or anal intercourse. It's ridiculous, we end up saying things like "up the front" or "up the back". I need you to tell me the slang terms. Then they'll know what we mean.'

'Well, you're not doing too badly,' I said, not quite sure how much time she had. This could end up being either a very long or a very short English lesson, but certainly unlike any other I'd given before. I could see from her expression, though, that it was important to her, so I pulled out my notebook and began writing what seemed likely to be the most common phrases, hoping that straightforward Anglo-Saxon would do the job.

'Suck,' the doctor said slowly as she watched me scribble. 'Cock.'

'That's a verb,' I said. 'This one's a noun.'

The obvious thing would have been to have talked to the Nigerians themselves and asked what terms they used, but it was early in the morning, Zine was waiting outside and I'd barely slept all night. The last thing I wanted was for them to think I was touting for business.

'Here,' I said, passing the piece of paper over when I'd finished. We went over the pronunciation for a few minutes while she took some notes, before I finally made my excuses.

'This is very, very helpful,' she said with a broad

smile, teeth stained with tobacco. 'We are trying to control disease here, but it is impossible if we cannot communicate with the girls. Thank you, thank you. Wonderful.'

And she looked down at the paper once again as I turned to leave, a silent but unmistakable mouthing of 'handjob' on her lips.

TARIFA

We reached Tarifa at dawn. I woke Zine with a nudge as a pink-grey light lifted from the sea, catching the tops of the hills then gradually working its way down the slopes. It was like watching a match burst into flame in slow motion. The towering mills of wind farms spread over the hillsides spun slowly and effortlessly, facing the wet south-west. Things were much greener here than I'd expected. We were considerably further south than the arid desert of Almería to the east, yet the pastoral scene reminded me of a sunnier version of Ireland, with rounded, treeless fields of grass, the occasional cow and an ever-present wind blowing off the Atlantic. To the west you could see what looked like rain clouds forming in the Bay of Cádiz.

When I first saw Africa I was convinced that my bearings had somehow got confused and I'd caught sight of some mountain range further towards Algeciras: the sea wasn't visible yet, and what I later realized to be Jabal Musa looked like an extension of the Spanish mainland, so close did it seem.

'Al-Maghrib,' Zine said dreamily. 'Morocco.'

Only when we got further down, and the silver-shifting seas came into view, did I recognize where we were. A whole massive, majestic continent stood before us like a magical world, as close and as distant as the cloud cities dreamt up in a child's imagination. You wanted immediately to reach out to it, to stretch out your hand and touch the untouchable, to cross this mirror-like barrier and enter into its different space. It seemed unnatural that there should be any division at all here, unnatural that either of us might belong or be rejected simply for being on one side or the other. This was a crossing-point, a gateway for both north and south and east and west, a geographical crossroads; not a wall for keeping people in or out. It was where the Islamic world had first touched Europe, where Tariq had brought his army of Arabs and Berbers: the birthplace of Al-Andalus. Landing in the spring of 711, Tariq had touched down at Gibraltar – *jabal Tariq* – before establishing his base across the bay on what he described as the 'green island', *al-jazira al-khadra*, today known as Algeciras. Five years later, the Muslims had conquered almost the entire peninsula, something the Romans had taken two centuries to achieve. And although there were no Muslims ruling here now, you could detect signs of their former presence in the white cubic houses of the villages, or dark Semitic faces, speaking a Latin tongue laced with words retained from when Arabic had been the spoken language here.

Tariq's invasion had not been the last southern force to cross the Strait: Berber armies of the Sahara had followed in his wake – Almoravids in the eleventh century, Almohads in the twelfth. They said that cannon had been used in Europe for the first time at

Algeciras in 1340, when Alfonso XI had besieged the Moorish-held city – although the technical innovation came from the defenders, not the attackers. Chaucer was to claim a role for his Knight in the successful siege.

Later, the invasions went in the opposite direction: the Portuguese in the fifteenth century, then the Spanish, claiming large parts of northern Morocco. To this day they still hold Ceuta, the southern sister of Gibraltar: an enclave of Christian Europe on the very tip of Africa.

More recently, the movement of peoples and conquest had pointed northwards once more: Franco had launched his ultimately successful assault on the Spanish mainland from the Moroccan side of the Strait in 1936, using, in typically paradoxical Spanish fashion, Moorish troops in his 'crusade' against the atheist Reds. While today, a largely invisible tide of immigrants was silently and secretly making its way over, risking everything in tiny overcrowded fishing boats to cross the deceptive waters and search for a better life in the prosperous north. I had one of them next to me in the car now.

'Is this where you came across?' I asked.

'Further over,' he said. 'Nearer Algeciras.'

'It looks closer than I imagined.'

'I can come and go as I please,' he said. 'Just like you.' I wasn't sure if he was bluffing, boasting or just dreaming aloud. I knew how hard it had been for him to come over, how much he missed Morocco. Weren't the Spanish girls he'd picked up his way of finding respite from loneliness? The man had smuggled himself away from home, only to be abused and enslaved. Now he was living off his wits, with no money, hitching a ride to what might turn out to be another dead-end job: a few weeks picking fruit, perhaps. No more. Nothing was certain in Zine's life. You couldn't condemn someone in his position.

We left the car by the side of the road on the outskirts of the town and walked down a dirt track towards the beach. The sun seemed to lift very slowly, taking its time to push away the night, as though hungover from the excesses of the day before. Zine still looked weak, and he lagged behind me a little on the path. The sea air would blow some freshness back into him, I thought. After our visit to the clinic in Seville, we'd wandered around the city trying to wake up, downing coffees in bars and taking refuge in the afternoon shade. The phone call to the girl in Granada had been short and, by the looks of things, curt: she'd already known she was infected when she'd had sex with him. Zine still looked unwell, but at least we knew he wasn't about to die. The day when we'd arranged to drop him off in Niebla at Uncle Sergio's had come upon us faster than we'd realized, and I'd wanted him to be as recovered as possible. And so I'd had the idea of bringing him down to the coast to see the southern tip of Spain at dawn – I'd always wondered if you could see Africa from here.

A quick stroll, some breakfast if he could manage it, and we could be in Niebla by lunchtime. I'd have to remember to give Uncle Sergio a call.

A fine spray-like fog was blowing in off the angry waves, while two tankers on an apparent collision course steamed headlong towards one another on the horizon. The water was so much more violent here on the Atlantic coast. I had grown used to the picture-postcard sea of the Mediterranean, with its elegant little waves, no tide and inviting temperatures. This, though, was a sea to be feared, great swells and troughs opening up as currents battled with one another above and below.

Zine walked away on his own for a while, his shoulders hunched and his head bent down against the wind. Sand and grit blew from where his footsteps disturbed it. It affected him more than he cared to admit, being so close here to Morocco. More so even than in Almería, where the country was just a concept, a memory, a possibility at the end of a ferry trip. Here it was staring him in the face. On a good day, I imagined you might even be tempted to swim to Africa just for fun, or row over and have a picnic. Except that you'd probably be shot at by over-zealous Spanish soldiers thinking you were out to invade some forgotten outcrop of rock they'd conquered back in the seventeenth century.

Turning away from the sea, I started following in Zine's footsteps, placing my feet in the holes he'd left in the sand, staring down at the stripy stones and shells that glistened with the salty water.

Zine spotted her first: I heard a yelp, partially muffled by the rushing noise of the sea, but enough to make me raise my eyes for a second. He was standing over a black heap of something, waving towards me with eyes like moons.

I ran over, slipping annoyingly as my feet failed to grip, my heart already sure of what my eyes were not.

The girl was naked save for a single white sock on her left foot. Her skin was wet and shining like the sea creatures washed up on the shore around her; her legs were doubled up under her in an unnatural position.

It was as though a single rejecting wave had coughed her up and landed her here halfway up the sand, breaking her like a doll. Her eyes were closed and her mouth hung open, as if she might snort or cough, change position and roll back to sleep on her other side. But she didn't move. There was no life left in her, no breath in her lungs. To be doubly sure I leant down and put my fingers to her throat, searching for a pulse, anything. Her young face was small and round, full cheeked, and her hair was braided back against her scalp. I couldn't really tell her age – eighteen? Twenty, perhaps. She looked West African, I thought. Guinean. It would have been a long journey already to get this far. And now nothing. Her naked flesh, so normal and natural on a beach, looked monstrous; it was ice-cold and already beginning to harden.

I turned away back to the sea, hot tears flooding my face. Seeing her was hard enough, but touching her deadness brought on a sudden, uncontrollable sorrow. Zine just stood still, eyes fixed on the girl, soft words from the Qur'an spilling from his mouth.

'*Qul a'udhu birrabi l-ghalaqi, min sharri ma ghalaqa* – I seek refuge in the Lord of Daybreak, from the evil of what He has created . . .'

Above our heads grey clouds like ink smudges on the pale-blue sky, edged with the pink light of dawn, moved in overland from the sea with heavy inevitability. Some dry orange peel and an empty packet of Fortuna cigarettes littered the ground by our feet, left by some happier bodies that had lain here once upon a time. Zine, I could tell, was looking at a version of himself, the Zine that never made it across the water a year before, but who drowned just as this girl had, perhaps capsizing after a freak wind, the boat

197

sinking under its own weight of people, or perhaps just cast off by the captain some two hundred yards or so from the shoreline – more than enough to be drowned in if you didn't know how to swim and the current was against you.

Turning back to look at the girl, I stood motionless next to Zine, the two of us frozen by the cold morning breeze, the icy spray coming off the waves and the horror of what lay before us.

Zine looked up at me.

'We need to tell someone,' I said.

He had an intense, resolute look on his face. Of course we should call the police straight away, but there was a problem.

'Jasie, perhaps I should just go now.' He looked back down at the girl on the sand. He knew: you didn't do this, you didn't just walk away from a corpse without doing something – even just a gesture. But Zine had to remain invisible if he were to stay in Spain. If we called the police now, the least that could happen to him would be an immediate ticket back to Tangier. But it could be a lot worse, as he'd already worked out.

'They might think *I* did this,' he said, his hand pointing at the body, then quickly drawing away, as though fearful of violating some sacred space that surrounded her. 'The men that do this, that bring these people over, are Moroccans,' he said, 'I've never heard of blacks crossing here – they usually go to the Canaries. But they'll think it was me. That I was the captain of the boat, or something.' He stopped for a moment, his mouth half-open with fear. 'I have to go. Now.'

He turned to leave.

'Zine, wait,' I called. 'Stop!' But he kept on walking,

moving up to the higher dunes where the sand was firmer.

I looked back down at the girl; her teeth were white against her blue skin. I had to do something for her, cover her up at least. But how was I going to do that apart from by digging a shallow sandy grave and making her harder to find when the police did come? Zine, meanwhile, was moving further away, his ringletted hair split by the wind. I couldn't let him disappear. He was on his own.

'Zine!'

He kept walking, unhearing in the sea wind. No way were they going to get him, not after everything else. As far as this – just an afternoon's drive from finally getting some work, within sight of the very land he'd left behind – and he was perhaps minutes away from losing every opportunity he had. From not only being sent back to Morocco, but the risk of imprisonment. The girl was dead; nothing could change that. He, though, was still alive, and needed to preserve what chances he had.

Making a snap decision, I ran up to the dunes, looking for something that might serve as a marker. I could make an anonymous call to the police, just not get involved. Grabbing a stick and a piece of bright-orange plastic washed up on the beach, I returned to the girl's body and made a makeshift flag, not much of a memorial but at least some recognition of what had happened here.

I caught up with Zine and grabbed him, and we ran back towards the car, our nerves jangling from not having slept for almost two days, and with the strange manic energy that seems to come with daybreak. Up here, away from the beach and the waves, it was as if none of this had happened. But the image of the girl's face was imprinted on my mind and I wouldn't be able to forget it.

Some minutes later we were driving into the centre of town looking for a phone box when we saw a Guardia Civil helicopter heading towards the beach. A couple of squad cars drove past; no sirens, but the men inside had fixed looks on their faces, as though they knew only too well what was waiting for them. Zine slid down in his seat and I hissed at him not to draw attention to himself.

The operator on the other end of the line took it very matter-of-factly, and seemed more concerned about me.

'*Lo siento por usted.*'

I gave her the details and hung up, but I was merely confirming what they already knew.

The complicated, contrasting colours of dawn had blanched into the usual white of midday as we headed back north – away from the coast, the view of Morocco, the body on the beach. Past two-tone cork oaks, bark stripped halfway, revealing the raw bloody brown flesh of the tree underneath. We were both exhausted and my hands shook slightly as they gripped the wheel. Zine tried to doze off, but his eyes refused to close, staring out unblinkingly at the road ahead.

'I'm sorry, Jasie,' he said. 'I'm sorry.'

NIEBLA

*W*e reached Niebla in the late afternoon. I rang Uncle Sergio, who gave us directions to his finca just north of the town. Zine and I exchanged a glance as we finally arrived at the farm. The earth felt thick underfoot, a smell of manure clinging to the air like cigarette smoke the morning after a long party.

'We'll have to take him to Javier's place,' Sergio said when I introduced him to Zine. 'Got no space for anyone here myself. But we'll find him something,' he added quickly when he saw my face drop. 'There's always work somewhere or other.'

He slapped me on the back.

'So you're the *novio* of my flamenco niece?' he said. 'She came down here and danced for us, ooh, about ten years ago. She had a concert on and called me up. "Uncle Sergio! I'm in Niebla." Ha! How's everyone back in Valencia? Haven't been there for years now.'

It was hard to believe this garrulous and cheery farmer was the younger brother of Salud's largely silent father. His neighbours still called him El Valenciano, yet he seemed at home in the south. Though why Sergio had chosen this forgotten corner of the country close to the Portuguese border, whiplashed by the Atlantic, was anyone's guess. But for the excellent serrano ham from the village of Jabugo half an hour's drive away, there was little to recommend it. To the north, the region of Extremadura had been the birthplace of many of the great Conquistadors of the New World – sweeping through Mexico and Peru must have been infinitely preferable to staying here. While on the coast just to the south was the town of Palos, the port from which Columbus made his first voyage across the Atlantic in 1492, just seven months after the fall of Granada. I got the impression this was a place most people were trying to get away from.

Columbus had planned his voyage at the monastery near Palos which stood on the site of a former Almohad religious retreat, from which it derived its name, La Rábida. An archway from the Moorish structure was still visible. He set sail in the *Santa María*, a sluggish and cumbersome square-rigged European *nau*. But also in his fleet were the *Pinta* and the *Niña*, both fast *caravels* – a lateen vessel used by the Arabs for centuries in the eastern Mediterranean. The name *caravel* came from the Arab *qarib*. Columbus would have used seafaring knowledge learned from the Moors, and was almost certainly aware of the work of medieval Arab cartographers such as Al-Idrisi – Arab geographers, influenced by the Alexandrine Ptolemy, had always said the Earth was a sphere. The astrolabes which he used to plot his course had been introduced to Europe via Spain some five hundred years earlier. Expecting to arrive in Asia on the other side of the Atlantic, Columbus took with him an Arabic-speaking Jew, Luis de Torres, to act as ambassador once they arrived. So it is possible that the first words spoken to American Indians by the Spanish conquerors were in Arabic. Ironic, as it was only because Granada had fallen earlier in the year that Queen Isabel agreed to back the voyage in the first place. Something of Moorish Spain had survived the military conquest and would play a part at the start of the new chapter in the country's history.

I took Zine back into Niebla for something to eat after we'd got him fixed up at Javier's farm. There was plenty of fruit picking to be done, and he set him up with one of the teams of workers that were inching their way through one of his fields. No acreage of white plastic here, I noticed with relief. I hadn't fancied taking Zine back into the conditions in which I'd found him, and I trusted Sergio and his friends to treat their workers decently.

We sat at a metal table at a bar with large windows overlooking the old red Moorish walls that ringed the town. They looked dusty and worn, like an octogenarian's favourite childhood toy lovingly brought down from years of storage to be given to an ungrateful grandchild. Neither of us spoke, the weight of what we had seen that morning still pressing on our minds. It isolated us, and made us feel apart from the buzzing life that surrounded us. Children were starting to pour out onto the pavement from the school opposite. The television, as in a thousand other Spanish bars, was on full blast, blaring out high-pitched nonsense.

'Where now?'

'Portugal,' I said.

He nodded, taking up a fork to pick at the potato and onion tortilla the barman had just placed on our table.

'What will you do?'

'Drive around; have a look. There are some people there I want to meet.'

He sighed, the skin above his nose folding as he tightened his brow. He'd found his job – the promise I'd made had been kept. Yet this didn't feel like the end even though the script said we had to part company here – he needed work and I needed to carry on. Much as I was tempted to, I knew it would be a mistake to suggest he keep travelling with me. The whole journey so far had been designed to bring him here.

The television blared more news of the build-up to conflict: the Pope had come out against an attack on Iraq, the Catholic government in Madrid sidestepping his comments awkwardly as the anti-war mood grew. People were warning of a humanitarian catastrophe.

'I think he's a good man, Javier,' Zine said after a pause. 'I can tell this is going to be better than the other farm.'

I laughed. 'It wouldn't take much to improve on that place.'

'And he doesn't carry a baseball bat, either.'

And so the decision was made: he was staying.

'Look,' I said as I drove him back, 'you've got my mobile number. If you . . .'

'It's all right, Jasie. I'll be fine. Perhaps I'll give you a ring if I'm ever back in Valencia.'

He smiled, but I felt sure that if we ever saw each other again it was more likely to be in Morocco.

'Give my love to Salud,' he said. 'And to Lucía.' His eyes fell with a look of sadness and resignation, the knot in his forehead tightening. 'She's a lovely girl.'

We got out of the car and embraced in the darkening evening air. He patted me on the cheek then turned and walked away — just a split-second too soon, a note of abruptness to a moment I had begun to think would never actually arrive.

THE SECRET MOSQUE

A madman ran the museum at Serpa, standing alone in the great moss-covered courtyard inside the old castle walls with half a dozen cats, wordlessly pointing things out in the rain to non-existent visitors. Sheltering under my umbrella, I skipped over the puddles towards the entrance: I couldn't tell if he'd seen me, so engrossed was he in explaining the structure of the phallic-shaped battlements to his invisible tourists. I'd seen the same design on the Arabic walls at Córdoba. A giant lump of the fortress hung precariously overhead, having been dislodged during a Spanish siege several hundred years earlier – it still hadn't fallen down completely, so it was left there: a reminder of the attack, but making the point that the invaders hadn't quite managed to destroy everything. It seemed very Portuguese, somehow.

On the upper floor of the museum I looked down onto the rest of the town, a muddle of white buildings and terracotta roofs squashed together within the limits of the ancient city walls. It was a quiet place: had it been a Spanish town, kids on scooters would have been riding down the wiggly streets at top speed, silencers removed from their exhaust pipes. Or music would be blaring from somewhere: dance music, pop. Noise of some sort. Here was just silence, even in the middle of the day. And it wasn't even lunch time.

Odd minaret-like chimneys rose from every house – tall cylinders capped with a dome and little stone ball on top, like the golden spheres that had once graced the Giralda in Seville, and which you could still see on her sister minaret in Marrakesh, the Kutubiyya. Geese, chickens and pigeons scrabbled among the gardens huddled at the foot of the castle defences, safe from the cats inside, sheltering from the downpour underneath lemon and fig trees, morning glories and Virginia creeper with the first shades of red showing in its leaves.

Across the square I could just make out the bar where the night before I'd eaten the most delicious fish stew – *sopa de cossão* – stuffed with coriander, garlic and lemon juice, slices of chewy bread floating on top. The Spanish had almost eradicated the use of coriander from their cooking, a herb the Moors used all the time – *kuzbara*, they called it; here its influence had lasted. I had been enjoying the meal, but for the bitter-tasting wine, when suddenly a ferocious middle-aged woman stormed into the restaurant looking for her husband. Just when I was beginning to think the Portuguese never made any noise at all.

'*PORCO!*' she screamed as she found him hiding in the kitchen, and landed a punch on his ear. The bar owner, clearly a friend of the poor man, made low-pitched groans of complaint, but the strangely cube-shaped jilted wife was in full flow.

'*PUTA! PORCO!*'

I thought some efforts would be made to shut her up, or at least move the marital dispute to a more private location. But no. Such displays of emotion appeared to be quite acceptable – the flip side of the coin from the usual haunting silence I'd encountered since entering the country. Portugal struck me as a fundamentally odd country: as though everyone here had had their testosterone levels artificially set to zero at birth. How else could you explain their languidness, moodiness, their melancholy and the nightly showing of the Women's Roller Hockey World Championship on primetime TV?

Some twenty minutes passed before the husband managed to escape the beating and fled to the toilet, where he locked himself in. The woman beat on the door a few times for good measure, called him a *porco* several times more, and then left, whispering an apologetic *disculpe* to me as she passed on the way out.

The Moors appeared to have left little evidence of their time in Portugal, and Serpa was no exception – a shard of an amphora was about as good as it got. But just as I was turning to leave the museum, a photograph in one of the display cabinets caught my eye. It showed a small dirty-white building, square and with a round dome on top – an unmistakable Moorish design. Underneath, a strip of paper pinned to the photo simply said 'Santa Margarida Mosque'. I looked back in my guidebook: there was no mention of such a place. And the man at the tourist information hadn't brought it to my attention either.

There was no clue to the whereabouts of the mosque.

I leant over to the window to peer into the courtyard, where the mad curator had been when I'd arrived: he was no longer there. I felt certain that somewhere inside that jumbled mind was the location of the Santa Margarida Mosque, so I set off to find him.

He crept up on me from behind as I went searching for him in the prehistoric section. With a start I turned round. His face was kind, skin like sandpaper, and, like most Portuguese men I'd seen, he wore a flat cap on his bony head.

'*Olá*,' he said. Just as in Spain, the greeting came from Allah, but with deeper Portuguese vowels it sounded even more like the original word. Zine would have had fun here, I thought.

'*Olá. Santa Margarida*,' I explained. '*A mesquita.*'

And then it began: the most bizarre set of instructions I'd ever heard, spoken in a garbled version of a language I already had difficulty understanding, and accompanied by huge sweeping arm movements and wild vibrating eyes. At times I thought I could pick out odd words of German or French. Just what language was the man speaking? Then he made the sounds of a river, birds twittering, a crunching noise as he jumped up and down. It was pure nonsense, but at the same time, and to my surprise, I started to understand what he meant: take the road to Beja, then turn off and cross a river bed, up a dirt track (the jumping up and down was the movement of a car driving on a bumpy road) and the mosque was in the middle of an orchard.

The effect of the man's wild gesticulations and gibberish-talk was to give me a crystal-clear image

211

of my route, as though he'd shown it to me on film.

And so fifteen minutes later I found myself outside the hidden Mosque of Santa Margarida, surrounded, as he'd told me, by olive trees filled with twittering birds, at the top of a slope on the other side of the muddy river bed from the Beja road. The mosque looked like a Second World War pillbox: a small greying structure with cracking walls covered in mildew, and a tiny green door. It was the spitting image of *zawiyas* you came across all over Morocco, and which could still be found in Spain: a quiet spot, perhaps marking the tomb of a holy man, or a solitary place of prayer; perhaps the meeting point for annual religious processions, when everyone marked a certain saint's day by walking out of town in a column to a sacred place in the country – *romerías*, they called them in Spain; *romarias* in Portugal, *moussems* in Morocco. Christian, Muslim: it didn't matter. Today they still called it a mosque, only it was dedicated to a Christian saint.

I tried the door, but it was locked. There was no one around. This part of Portugal, the Alentejo, was supposedly the poorest region in Europe: people were a rare commodity. I tried again, but still it refused to open; I might have tried harder but I didn't want to have break-in and entry into a mosque/church on my conscience. After circling round it a couple of times I realized that there was no way in, and nobody was on hand with the key. Probably empty, I thought in an attempt to console myself. Finding it in the first place was the important thing.

It started raining again and I headed back to the car. Although deep inland and almost on the Spanish border, you felt the presence of the Atlantic in the rapid shifts of weather blowing in off the ocean: rain, then searing humid heat, strong winds, then more rain.

It was time to go. The inside of the mosque would have to remain a mystery.

MÉRTOLA

'*B*iologists say we're genetically very close to North Africans. They want to set up an organ donation programme between Portugal and Morocco.'

Santiago Macias could barely have looked less Moorish, with his fair hair and distractingly blue eyes. His family, he told me, was originally from northern Spain, exiles from Franco. But the Lusophone Santiago now chatting to me over a bottle of mineral water and a cigarette had become one of the leading lights of the nascent field of Islamic studies in Portugal – a far more politically charged affair than anything I'd come across in Spain.

You had to look back to the dictatorship of Salazar to understand the importance of what Santiago and his main collaborator Claudio Torres, the godfather of Arab studies in Portugal, were doing.

António de Oliveira Salazar had been the most low-key of Europe's fascist leaders. A celibate former economics professor, he had neither the theatricality of Mussolini, the evil of Hitler nor the enigmatic guile of Franco, yet he ruled Portugal virtually single-handedly from 1932 to 1968. Catholic and austere, he drew on a romanticized view of the Portuguese Reconquest and the Age of Exploration to create a pageant-like imagery to legitimize his regime. The result was that for decades Arab studies were almost non-existent in the country – in what appeared to have been a more extreme version of what had happened in Spain, the Moorish period of Portugal's history was simply rubbed out in favour of a picture of Christian purity, and no archaeological digs which might show to the contrary were allowed.

Things only began to change after Salazar died. The man who spearheaded events was Claudio Torres, a former Communist activist who had concentrated his efforts in the ancient Alentejo hilltop village of Mértola. Apart from his more academic work, he had also revived and promoted traditional crafts that dated back to Moorish times, such as the weaving of brown and white woollen blankets with intricate geometric patterns. The idea had caught on: other Arabists, including Santiago, had come to join the Mértola project, and the place had become Portugal's main centre of investigation into the Moorish past.

Set at the joining of two rivers, the tiny, bustling village had the feeling of another era to it – mounted policemen with big moustaches in grey, military-style uniforms looking like something from a hundred years ago, children shuddering down cobbled streets on push-bikes and foot-scooters. Buildings were painted in bright clean colours – a sky-blue star framing a white window, heavy fire-engine-red doors at the entrance to a nineteenth-century public building. Old women covered their hair with black scarves tied underneath their chins and straw hats balanced on top of their heads, as in many parts of Morocco. Zine would have looked more like a local than he did in Spain, I thought. Complexions were generally dark, but in addition, many men had tight-knotted, almost Afro hair, the kind so common among North Africans. On four or five occasions I'd mistaken Portuguese walking in the street for Moroccan immigrants, only realizing they were local when I heard them speak.

The surrounding landscape was like something from a Chinese watercolour, with steep valleys, tall delicate trees and waterfalls – the whole scene painted in shades of green and grey. The church was a former mosque – easily identified by its rectangular shape and rows of columns. And below the walls of the old castle that crowned the village was a small chapel – again a former Islamic building with its tell-tale cubic structure topped with a dome like an orange sliced in half. Inside was kept a very hairy-looking statue of Jesus, with demonic black eyes.

'Mértola was an economic disaster in the Middle Ages. That's why we're based here, because the place has effectively been preserved,' Santiago told me, speaking in almost flawless English. 'Lisbon and Beja were more important for the Moors, but very little remains.'

Working men wearing flat caps came into the bar where we were sitting, their skin rough and dry, their bodies heavy and burdensome. One of them had a lump the size of an apple on the back of his neck. Poverty appeared to be afflicting the region even now.

There seemed a genuine love of his subject behind what Santiago said, and I quickly warmed to his enthusiasm and friendliness: I'd only called him up to arrange the meeting fifteen minutes beforehand and he'd agreed to come round without any hesitation.

'You're lucky to have found me,' he said. 'I'm supposed to be at a conference in Lisbon today. I have to leave in an hour.'

I explained the reason I was there, and my search.

'The legacy of the Moors in Portugal is more subtle in some ways than in Spain,' Santiago told me. 'Here there is no Alhambra or Córdoba Mosque, yet the link is strong. Lisbon, for example, is closer to Rabat than Madrid.'

I was struck by this idea, which had never occurred to me before, and I made a mental note to check it when I got back to the car. Although, as it turned out, Madrid had it by a few miles, the point was clear – North Africa was closer than it seemed.

'The Mértola project has been ongoing for over fifteen years now. The mosque is obviously an important site, but we've also found graves with Islamic inscriptions next to Christian ones – people were buried together. The whole village is dotted with them – nothing spectacular in themselves, but the significance of finding something like this after years of denying the Moors were ever a serious presence in the country is enormous.'

Santiago went on to explain why.

The Moorish conquest had been more like an assimilation than the rapid invasion described in the history books. No Islamic tombs had yet been found from before the eleventh century. Essentially the same people were here before and after the Arabs arrived – they just became Muslims.

On the TV news the night before there'd been footage of mass arrests of Al-Qa'ida suspects in Lisbon. The police chief in charge of the operation was interviewed afterwards and looked as Arabic as the people he'd just detained: olive skin, thick mouth, strong round chin and black curly hair.

'We Portuguese pride ourselves on not being racist,' Santiago said when I mentioned this to him. 'But it's not entirely true: northerners call the people of the south *mouros*. And they're not being polite.'

Just as in Italy, where northerners often called the toe of the peninsula Calabria Saudita – Saudi Calabria.

Yet there were about six hundred words from Arabic in Portuguese, even though some of them were being lost as society and the language evolved. *Falua*, for example, came from the Arabic for 'little horse' and was used in Portugal to describe a certain kind of small boat. But those boats were no longer used, so the word was dying out. The same went with old measurements – the Arabic terms were lost with the switch to litres and grams. The Portuguese had *oxalá*, like *ojalá* in Spanish. And then there was the expression *Deus é grande!*, taken from *Allahu akbar* – God is great – in Arabic. You had to look for the influence in subtle things like this, Santiago said, the language of food, for example – all the *escabeche* sauces in the Algarve made from vinegar. There were similar dishes in Spain, where anything from rabbit to sardines could be prepared in thick onion and vinegar gravy.

'Then there's the Alfama district of Lisbon,' he continued. 'The name comes from the Arabic *al-hammam* – bath house.'

According to Claudio, his colleague, you could hear Moorish influences in the mournful sounds of the local Alentejo choirs, or see it in the designs woven into the blankets the women made, or the fact that in Portuguese they gave the days of the week numbers rather than names, just as in Arabic: Day One, Day Two.

'We're surrounded by this kind of thing. Have you seen the Marrakesh-style battlements on top of the church? It's everywhere. And then there are the stories of the Moorish Maiden.'

I sat up. 'What stories?'

'Oh, it's a kind of national legend. Some say a Moorish maiden helped the knights of Santiago reconquer the southern town of Aljezur – the last to be taken by the Christians – by secretly opening the city gates in the middle of the night. Then others say she's a ghost collecting water, crying because the Moors are no longer in Portugal.'

He stubbed out his cigarette.

'And then there's the story about a shepherd who saw some amazing light while he was out with his sheep.'

Legend had it the shepherd walked towards the light and saw a beautiful Moorish woman surrounded by jewels and treasure, and she called out to him: 'Come. Take all the gold you want, but whatever you do, don't tell anyone about this, and more importantly, don't look back when you walk away.' And so this is what the shepherd did. He picked up all the gold that he could and ran off back down the mountainside. But halfway down he looked back to see this light just one more time, even though the woman had told him not to. And when he got home he told everyone about what had happened. When he returned to the place where he'd found the gold, all he saw was rusty scrap metal. And so today – according to the story – you can still find many pieces of this old metal left behind by the shepherd, scattered over the hilltop.

Santiago lit another cigarette as I finished copying the story down.

'They're stories grandmothers tell,' he said, as though it was of little importance. I nodded and remained silent as I felt another piece of the puzzle slot into place. This was the same legend as Musa the Moor and his hidden treasure, the tale that had made me start on all of this in the first place. Portugal's Moorish Maiden was the same person as Zoraida, the daughter of the legendary ruler of Al-Andalus, guarding her father's treasure from the unworthy by making it appear less valuable than it actually was. In Spain it was stones: here it was pieces of rusty metal.

'There's another thing you must have seen too,' Santiago said when I looked up. 'The Hand of Fatima.'

I had noticed that dozens of door-knockers were in the shape of a woman's hand holding a ball, a ring on her second or third finger.

'That's another Moorish legacy. It's to ward off the evil eye.'

'Isn't the Virgin of Fatima the patron of Portugal?' I asked.

'Yes, that's because of the three children who saw visions of Mary in the village of Fatima during the First World War. Salazar turned her into an icon.' He lowered his voice for a comic pompous effect. 'The saviour of Portugal.'

'It seems Fatima's a common name here, just like in the Middle East,' I said.

'That's right,' he laughed as he got up from the table. 'But it's just coincidence.' He shook my hand. 'I have to leave now. I'm so sorry. But I have to get to Lisbon. Good luck with your journey.'

Coincidence. But as I watched him step out of the bar back into the humid sun of the village square, I found the treasure-seeker in me liked the idea that the very man who'd denied the country's Arab past had venerated a holy woman with the same name as Muhammad's daughter.

In the past they had buried Muslims and Christians together; now Salazar's efforts to bury the mixed Muslim-Christian culture of his own country for good were coming to nought.

It was a slippery thing, this Moorish legacy.

BELMONTE

'This is my spiritual home. Cleveland Ohio's where I was born and where I live, but this is where I *really* belong.'

Esther smelt of adrenaline, a piece of chewing gum relentlessly pummelled between her jaws. Her heavy thighs were pressed out flat against the low granite wall where we sat near the village square. She was taking a momentary break from her tour group as they took photos of the monument to Pedro Álvares Cabral, the discoverer of Brazil and the most famous son of the tiny village of Belmonte.

'This is just tourist stuff,' she said, pointing to the massive green-bronze statue of the famous explorer, who clutched his sword, astrolabe and a cross about twice the size of him. It reminded me of fascist sculpture of the thirties: simplistic and just slightly over-dramatic. There was a theory that Cabral hadn't been the first to reach Brazil, but rather a group of Berbers from the Barazil tribe who had arrived there a few hundred years before, hence the name of the country. But she seemed uninterested in this side of Belmonte's history, and focused solely on the reason for her visit.

I pulled my jacket closer around my body: high in the mountains on the Portuguese–Spanish border autumn had come on rather suddenly, despite the pale, cloudless sky above. Church bells rang out in the silence of a largely deserted village, while my stomach protested at the sausage roll I'd picked up for lunch at a local pastry shop. The landscape reminded me of the north of England – all moss-covered drystone walls and sodden fields.

'We had dinner with the rabbi last night. It was so special. I've been planning this trip for twenty years, ever since Mom told us about our Sephardic past. I mean, I knew I was Jewish, but I had no idea about what happened to us here, about the Inquisition and everything. They threw everyone out. Can you believe that?'

I wondered why it had taken so long for her to fly to Portugal and take the three-hour ride to Belmonte, but my question got lost on the tidal wave of emotion.

'These people, they hid their Jewishness for FIVE HUNDRED YEARS. I mean, like, wow! How d'you do that? How d'you keep your faith secret for *so* long? While everywhere they're burning people at the stake just because they *look* Jewish. It's mind-blowing. I'm just like, wow. I knew I had to come here. I've been waiting for this for so long, and it's just like, yeah, this is it. This is home. This is my home.'

Eighty-five years had passed since the crypto-Jewish community of Belmonte had first been discovered by the outside world, when Samuel Schwartz, a visiting Polish mining engineer, had spoken to them the only Hebrew word they had retained after four centuries in hiding: *A-donai*, 'Lord'. Until that moment they had

227

thought they were the only Jews left in the world; while the world thought not a single Jew remained from the time when the Iberian Peninsula was once regarded as a second Jerusalem. Viewed as perhaps an eccentric group within the village, the Belmonte *marranos* had made a show of Catholicism in the relative safety of the border region, far from the centre of the Inquisition in Lisbon, hiding their true religion and as much of their culture as they possibly could from the murderous authorities. Out of a population of hundreds of thousands, a people that produced philosophers, poets, ministers and craftsmen, this group of some two hundred people were all that remained of the Jews who had once lived throughout Spain and Portugal.

The first Jews had arrived on the peninsula in the first century AD – perhaps even before – and they called this land at the far western end of the Mediterranean Sefarad, from which came the word Sephardic. Persecuted by the Visigoths, they had welcomed the Muslim invaders of the eighth century as liberators, and went on to play a vital role in the cultural and political life of Al-Andalus. Maimonides, the great Jewish philosopher and author of the *Guide for the Perplexed*, one of the most important works in Judaism after the Talmud and the Torah, had been born in Córdoba; and Jewish culture underwent a renaissance during the Moorish period: Ibrahim bar Hiyya, a Barcelona-based mathematician, wrote the first Hebrew encyclopaedia in the twelfth century – the *Yesod ha-Tebunah u-Migdal ha-Emunah*; the Catalan city of Gerona had been a major centre of Cabbalah mysticism and had even been known as the 'Mother City of Israel'; while Tarragona had been almost entirely Jewish in Moorish times – when the Christian Ramón Berenguer IV conquered it in the mid twelfth century, he had a new cathedral built almost entirely by Jewish architects, using 'Islamic' designs.

As the Christian areas of Spain had grown, so the position of the Jews had changed. Generally tolerated as they were by Muslims at first, there was an eventual order for their expulsion in 1492, just months after Isabel and Ferdinand had conquered Granada. Many left for North Africa and other parts of the Mediterranean, forever exiled and speaking a fifteenth-century form of Spanish – Ladino – that has survived to this day. But many others chose to stay, forced to convert to Catholicism in order to remain in what had been their people's homeland for some fifteen hundred years.

Converts often suffered as much as those who chose to go into exile. Perhaps more. Suspected of practising Judaism in secret, they were commonly referred to as *marranos*, 'dirty swine'. It was this community, and the 'problem' it represented – heresy, a 'secret' group within society – which became the first target of the Spanish Inquisition. The Holy Office began operating in 1481 with the main intention of policing the beliefs of this new, rapidly growing section of the population.

The odds were against you if Inquisitors came knocking on your door: people were never told who their accuser was, and torture to extract a 'confession' was common: hanging prisoners upside down, forcing them to drink vast amounts of water, or stretching them on the rack. Too often the process ended at the stake – the infamous autos-da-fé.

The Inquisition burnt people fairly systematically for some three hundred years, doing its best to obliterate Jewish and later Moorish culture from Spanish life. For a long time the worst insult in Spain was to accuse somebody of having 'mixed' blood. The seventeenth-century play *Fuente Ovejuna* by Lope de Vega includes a scene where a country peasant makes fun of a nobleman, saying that as he comes from the city, he is far more likely to have Jewish or Moorish ancestors.

Even now Spanish people recognize, if not use, the phrase *hacer una judiada* – literally 'to do a Jewish-type thing', meaning something bad or nasty. Traditional proverbs used to go even further: *El judío cuando al cristiano no puede engañarle más, escupe en la sombra por detrás* – When a Jew can't cheat a Christian any more, he spits on his shadow when his back is turned.

For centuries the Jews of Belmonte had survived in their mountain hideaway, escaping detection by eating *alheira* sausages made from smoked chicken instead of pork – no one could taste the difference; they celebrated Jewish feasts such as Passover a day or so after the official date, so as to confuse the Inquisitors; they hid their Shabbat lamps in clay pots, making sure all the doors and windows were closed so no one could look in; and they had women lead their services. On entering a church they would utter a secret phrase affirming they 'only adored the God of Israel'. They refused to light fires or work on Saturdays, and at Yom Kippur women from the community would continue the practice of gathering to braid oil wicks while reciting seventy-three blessings. Schwartz once saw a *marrano* merchant arguing with a client from out of town over the price of something. It was Friday night, and they didn't reach a deal. After dinner, the buyer had second thoughts and decided to accept the merchant's price, but the merchant refused to do any business with him. They next day he tried again, but still the answer, no. 'Come back tonight!' the Jewish merchant said. Despite his growing doubts about the man, the buyer returned later and the merchant sold him the goods – at a lower price. As Schwartz later explained to the confused buyer, the merchant was behaving according to Sabbath practices, even if he wasn't completely aware why.

'Are you Jewish too?' Esther asked me. Blond and blue-eyed as I was, I had once thought I was about as physically unJewish as one could possibly be. But on a trip to Jerusalem I'd been asked the same question several times, so had begun to revise my ideas.

'It's just so wonderful to know these people are here,' Esther went on. 'To know they survived. That's ... that's *really* powerful. I mean, the Portuguese treated them awful.'

Esther explained that Jews had arrived in Portugal from Spain to escape the Inquisition, but that three years later the Portuguese had begun their own persecution and thrown them out too. Her family had eventually ended up in Thessalonika, but centuries later had left for the United States, just before the war.

A good job, too, I thought. The Nazis had almost obliterated the Sephardic community in northern Greece. The Portuguese treatment of the Jews, as in Spain at the same time, had been appalling, perhaps one of the worst disasters to befall the Jewish community before the Final Solution. On the face of it, the Inquisition had succeeded – Spain and Portugal were avowedly Catholic countries, where for centuries anything like free thought had been all but wiped out.

Only places like Belmonte hinted at the fact that not everything was as it seemed.

'Where're you from, Jason?' Esther asked.

I explained: born in the US; English parents; years living in Germany, Italy and Spain; a spell or two in the Middle East. Sometimes I felt different parts of me belonged to every one of these places.

'Oh, I *know* how complicated a question it can be. I'm American, sure. Jewish. But Greek? Portuguese? Spanish? There's some Lithuanian in me somewhere too.' She laughed and looked down at herself, as though searching for the answer in some part of her anatomy. Then she breathed in deeply. 'You know, I think perhaps I'm just Belmontese.'

Across from where we were sitting the rest of the tour group were talking in twos and threes, almost everyone dressed in the uniform of jeans, white running shoes and sunglasses. The tour leader – a Portuguese-looking woman in her forties with dark skin and wide-open eyes – was explaining something about the hotel they were staying at that night.

I asked how the Jewish people in the village seemed to her.

'Still shy and secretive,' she said. 'We came on an organized trip. We've got historians and all kinds of people with us – they've been studying them for years!' She raised a finger up in my face to accentuate the point. 'But, hey! So would you be careful if they'd been burning your relatives at the stake for centuries.'

The Inquisition had been a devastating episode of ethnic cleansing, with people arrested for all kinds of trivial things, like not eating pork, or just washing yourself – something the Church at the time didn't look favourably upon. After working on the Jewish community, the Inquisitors turned their attention to Moors, and then ordinary Christians with a less than perfectly orthodox attitude.

'They even charged some woman because they overheard her say, "If my husband ever gets into Heaven then so will donkeys," ' I said.

'Wow. Was she Jewish?'

'Just an ordinary Christian. But they thought it was blasphemous. They had three hundred years of that kind of thing. You don't recover from that overnight. Maybe never at all.'

One of the historians on Esther's tour had explained that the Inquisition did make it to Belmonte. The village Jewish community often claimed the Holy Office never made it up into the mountains, but the historian said documents from the time showed that in fact it had reached this isolated spot.

'These people must have been *really* brave. To live through that! I just feel so good being here: it makes me feel proud.'

A couple of men from the village, dressed in cardigans and corduroy trousers, walked past mumbling to one another, sounding, like most Portuguese I'd come across, like drunk Russians trying to speak Spanish. A friend in Lisbon had told me the Ukrainian immigrants had perfect accents. Something about the lugubriousness of the Portuguese reminded me of east Europeans sometimes.

'I've heard,' I said to Esther in a low voice, 'that some of the Jewish people here aren't entirely happy about being discovered. That they were all right without a synagogue or a rabbi, and that all this attention and change has caused some problems.'

She leant towards me, quickly falling into the role of

fellow conspirator, the gum in her mouth awarded momentary respite.

'You know, I'd heard the same. I didn't like to say anything, but I think some aren't too happy about being Orthodox. A group of them formally converted about ten years ago – some guy aged eighty had a circumcision done. Can you believe that?'

Having been snipped myself in a Californian hospital after a mere day in the world as a complete human being, I could empathize to a point. In fact, the Spanish Jew Maimonides was in part responsible, having asserted in his *Guide* that circumcision was generally a good thing: 'Circumcision simply counteracts excessive lust,' he said. 'The organ necessarily becomes weak when it loses blood.'

During the nineteenth century conservative Christians in the US, including one John Harvey Kellogg, the inventor of the cornflake, had picked up on Jewish ideas – stemming largely from Maimonides – in a puritanical attempt to prevent masturbation and fornication. 'No foreskin, no foreplay,' was kind of how they reasoned. Of course, it didn't work, as I could personally testify, but the practice had been handed down to the present day under the pretext of 'physical' if not so much 'moral' hygiene. Yet the link was clear: thanks to some philosophizing Andalusi busy-body I wasn't quite whole – living proof of how far the legacy of Moorish Spain could extend.

The women of the village had sung songs and passed them down to their daughters, Esther continued. It was a way of life, and now it was all in the open. 'They have a new synagogue. Did you see it? Oh, you should go: it's beautiful.'

But the new rabbi had been telling them they

couldn't sing the old songs any more, or worship amalgamated holy men they'd invented like St Moses.

'I mean, of course: they were isolated for centuries – you forget some things, you make up some others. The church had to have an influence, no matter how hard they tried to remain Jewish at home.'

'Do you think it's better this way?' I asked. 'That Orthodox Judaism has arrived?'

'Oh, that's a *really* difficult question. You should talk to them about it.' And she smiled.

The rest of the group were gathering their things as they started moving off for the next stop on their tour. Esther lifted herself off the granite wall and made to shake my hand.

'It was very nice meeting you.'

I'd enjoyed our chat and was about to suggest we swap addresses, but before I had a chance she was already halfway up the square, walking quickly in her movement-restricting trousers to catch up with the other Americans finding 'home' here.

I was an American too, or at least I had a birth certificate that said so. Yet I felt as much an outsider here as anywhere, both in Portugal and with the American tour group. How did the Belmonte Jews feel, I wondered? Members of a wandering people who had disguised themselves to remain in a country that was both their home and a foreign land. Now other Jews were telling them they weren't properly Jewish at all. Perhaps by staying put and not leaving with the other exiles in the fifteenth century they'd foregone some essential part of themselves. How could 'home' be somewhere that rejected you so? The place felt like a kind of strange, inverted prison.

As I sat there I found my thoughts turning to Zine.

He could only leave home and wander in the first place by going in disguise. He'd talked about Morocco sometimes as a place difficult to get out of, somewhere they always wanted to send you back to. Home. But at the same time he was as homeless as I was.

Some fighting to escape; others fighting to remain. I had the feeling of going round in circles. Perhaps it wasn't a question of 'fighting' in the first place.

I decided to give Zine a call, perhaps the following day, when I'd be back over the border in Spain. At least try and get word of him from Uncle Sergio. For now, though, I thought it better to leave the Belmonte Jews in peace.

TOLEDO

Zine stood out from the others in the crowd, deep-brown eyes set wide apart and slightly protruding, with an intensity that drew your attention to them.

I saw him first, amid the elderly ladies and bony trees of the Zocodover, the site of the old Arab horse market, or *souq al-dawabb*, and still the heart of the modern city. A group of some two hundred people were walking haphazardly round in a circle waving colourful banners in the damp misty air, shouting a slogan to the beat of a solitary drum.

'*¡NO A LA GUERRA! ¡NO A LA GUERRA!*' Tum tum ti tum.

I hadn't expected to find much anti-war sentiment in a place like Toledo, where furs, high heels and Loden coats were the norm, the typical badges of the Spanish Right. This was the centre of 'old Spain' – the former capital of the country in pre-Moorish days: a small, dark medieval town that had barely changed since El Greco lived and painted here in the sixteenth century, and was still the headquarters of the Catholic Church in Spain. Two hundred yards up the road stood the Alcázar (Arabic: *al-qasr*) – the monolithic fortress on the crest of the hill on which the city was built: the site of the rebels' greatest hour in the Spanish Civil War, when a handful of defenders held out against the Republican siege for two months until Franco diverted his push on Madrid to relieve them, winning a propaganda victory but extending the war by another couple of years in so doing. Now, though, there was just a scent of change, with a poll in that morning's paper showing that over ninety per cent of the population opposed the right-wing government's decision to support the US in its build-up for war in Iraq. The Spanish, famed – wrongly – for being a bloodthirsty race, were breaking long-standing rules of behaviour over a war that no one here wanted.

I watched him for as long as I could before he caught sight of me. It was odd that I felt no surprise at seeing him there. His hair was shorter, no longer the ringlets circling around his ears, but it felt as though we had merely separated that morning and were now rejoining at midday for lunch and to make plans for the afternoon; not the fortnight since I'd last seen him. And now he was here it felt as if a missing order had been restored. A smile began forming at the corners of my mouth.

'Jasie!'

'Come on,' I said. And I took him to sit at one of the cafés that lined the square: it would be easier to talk over hot cups of milky coffee, rather than shouting against the rattle of the march.

Heavy leaden crows were scuffling among the yellowing treetops as elderly couples pushed through the thickening fog that was filling the Zocodover. Across from our café an old government building betrayed just a glimpse of the greatness of the city's past with a horseshoe archway tucked away inside the shadow of the entrance hall behind the standard neo-classical façade. Visitors came to the city to see El Entierro del Conde de Orgaz, and to admire the two medieval synagogues: relics from a more tolerant age. Some might even make it to the mosque, one of the oldest remaining in Spain. Today it was called the Church of Cristo de la Luz, the Christ of Light, an aptly abstract and iconic dedication for a former Islamic place of worship. Its interlacing red-brick archways were clearly reminiscent of the Great Mosque in Córdoba, and were repeated a thousand times in the *mudejar* structures around us that most typified Spanish medieval architecture – buildings put up under Christian rule by Moorish builders in the Islamic style. But there was no building or monument that symbolized Toledo's greatest gift to the Western world, perhaps the single most important jewel in the legacy of Al-Andalus: the school of translators.

In 1085 King Alfonso VI conquered Toledo, a city in which he himself had previously been given refuge by the Moorish rulers during fraternal in-fighting at the Castillian court. For the following two hundred years it became the intellectual capital of Christian Europe, a concentration point through which learning from the Islamic world passed into the West. As the main centre for translation into Latin of Arabic and Greek science, it laid the essential groundwork for the Renaissance. Europe in the Dark Ages had lost touch with Classical learning – Greek was virtually unknown. As Arab, Jewish and Christian scholars in Toledo reintroduced a wealth of Greek texts – Plato, Aristotle, Ptolemy: writings we take entirely for granted now – the

Classical world became available for 'rediscovery' later on. No Toledo, no Florence.

The Moorish role in this was crucial: Greek texts had been preserved by being translated into Arabic in the ninth century in Baghdad. It was from these manuscripts, then, that the Toledo scholars worked, translating from a translation into Latin.

Just as importantly, though, the Toledo school also translated a huge body of mathematical, philosophical, medicinal and scientific scholarship from the Arabic corpus, much of which had been built on Greek learning, but which combined elements from all over the Islamic empire and beyond. Hi-tech knowledge about astrolabes and abacuses had already seeped through into Europe from Al-Andalus, thanks partly to the magician Gerbert, later Pope Sylvester II, who travelled to Moorish Spain as a young man seeking 'wisdom'. Now, though, came concepts such as 'algebra', from the Arabic *al-jabr* – 'the bringing together of broken parts' – and 'logarithms', named after their Afghan originator Al-Khwarizmi. Arabic numbers also arrived, adapted in Baghdad from the Indian numerical system, and including the revolutionary concept of 'zero', from the Arabic *sifr*.

The 'school' of translators, originally gathered around the Archdeacon of Segovia Dominico Gundesalvo, a Christian Jew, was in fact a largely unstructured movement under church patronage that lasted for some 150 years, converting as much of the body of knowledge on the other side of the religious divide as possible into a more accessible format. The school itself, however, was a model of *convivencia*, an example of Moors, Christians and Jews coming together peacefully in cultural and intellectual pursuit. The translators would work in teams: an Arab speaker – sometimes a Muslim, sometimes a Jew – rendering the text into vernacular, i.e. early Castillian Spanish; a Christian scholar would then turn this into Latin.

The story of one of these Christian scholars – Gerard of Cremona – gave a feel for the kind of place Toledo was in those times. Gerard arrived in 1140 looking for a copy of Ptolemy's *Almagest*, having been unable to find one in his native Italy. Amazed at the wealth of material available in the city, he stayed, learnt Arabic and ended up translating over seventy books into Latin: twenty-four on medicine; eighteen on astronomy and alchemy; seventeen on maths; eleven on philosophy; and three on logic.

'In this way,' his students wrote of him when he died in Toledo some fifty years later, 'he passed on the Arabic literature in the manner of the wise man who, wandering through a green field, links up a crown of flowers, made not just from any, but from the prettiest. To the end of his life he continued to transmit to the Latin world, as if to his own beloved heir, whatever books he thought finest, in many subjects, as accurately and plainly as he could.'

'It was a good farm,' Zine began. 'Much better than the other – where you found me. They paid us in cash at the end of every day based on how many crates of fruit we'd filled. Then we were free to go; I went with some other Moroccans to a shelter near by – it was that or sleeping rough near the bus station. You saved money that way, but I didn't fancy it.'

Several months afterwards, his decision appeared all the wiser when, in an apparently random act of violence, three Moroccans living in the open in that same area were beaten up; one of the victims later died of his injuries.

'They didn't segregate us like on the other farm – there were a couple of Ukrainians on our team, and some Poles. And four Moroccans: a man from the Rif in his forties and two kids from Tetouan. I used to stick with the Rifian – he was from Chaouen. I have an aunt who lives there – I stayed with her once. The Chaounis are tough people: I like them. So we used to talk, the Rifian and I. His wife was pregnant with their third child. There was no work at home, so . . .'

There was a momentary silence and I could tell he was thinking of the girl on the beach in Tarifa. The waiter placed our drinks on the table, sweeping the crumbs left by the previous occupants onto the floor with a single motion of a damp cloth.

'I thought: this is someone I should listen to,' Zine continued. 'He had no fear, this man. He did what needed to be done. He needed work, his wife was pregnant, so he went and found work. It was the third time he'd been in Spain. They'd thrown him out twice before, but he just came back whenever he could and earned money until they got hold of him again. He didn't care. It didn't matter. He told me, anyway, the Spanish police are usually very friendly. They send you back home but they look after you while you are with them. I think this is very Spanish. It is the *moro* in them.'

I laughed.

'I thought you'd like that. Their humanity comes from us, from their Moorish cousins. All this business about war in Iraq. Look outside. These people know it is wrong. But the government is crazy.'

Outside the rhythmic chant of the demonstrators ebbed and flowed as customers came in and out through the café door. A left-wing party seemed to be organizing things, but I was surprised to see passers-by stopping and reading leaflets being handed out, standing on the edge as though thinking about joining in. Only a few months later, on the eve of war itself, many of them would actually do so.

'How did you know I was in Toledo?' I asked.

'I called Salud,' he said, amused that I should be puzzled by something so straightforward. 'She said you were here.'

'And how did you get here?'

'I got a lift with a lorry driver from the farm.'

In the back of my mind I could hear Salud laughing.

'I need to be like that Rifian,' he said with force. 'With no fear.'

Now I really was surprised. This was Zine, who had left home and risked his life crossing the Strait of Gibraltar to find work in a foreign inhospitable country, who had risked it again by saving me from the slave farm, throwing away his only chance of work. Zine the orphan, who had such an easy way with women. Zine, who I thought of as anything but fearful. And yet just as clearly, as he spoke those words, I felt I'd understood: not only something about him, but about myself too. We were both trying to overcome fears within ourselves. One of the first things he'd said to me was that fear was meaningless when you knew life itself came to an end. But wasn't that what we were both trying to prove to ourselves: that we had beaten fear? Taking off, an adventure, life on the road: it was as if we needed daily reassurance that we were no longer frightened – in his case of coming to Spain and leaving Morocco in the first place; in mine, of remaining here for good.

'My uncle, the one who took me in when my parents died, has an export business in Casablanca. He runs it with my two cousins. They wanted me to join when I left school – or at least my uncle did. My cousins, I don't know. I agreed, but as soon as I could I left. I said I wanted to visit other members of my family – that's how I went to Chaouen, and then ended up in Tangier. I told them I was making business contacts there. I stayed with a sister of my mother's. My uncle thought all this would be useful later on when I eventually went to work with him. But I – we didn't get on. My uncle never liked my mother: he didn't like my father marrying a Berber.'

For all the time I had known him I had held back from asking too much about Zine's past. I instinctively felt I should simply listen to what he wanted me to know. Exiles I'd met in the past were often a complex of closed doors, who reacted unfavourably to people pushing too hard to get through. Zine had been no exception. And though not on the run from his home country, he was considered an 'illegal' in the land to which he'd chosen to come. Secrets were part of surviving. And fear as well: I could see that now.

'I was in Tangier for seven years,' he said. 'My aunt, my mother's sister, is married to a schoolteacher. They called me . . .' He paused. 'You know . . . *khuffash*.'

'A bat?'

'Yes, they called me "the bat" because I was always out at night, never seeing where I was going. Going here, then there. All over. I wanted to leave Casablanca and my uncle, so I went to Tangier. Then in Tangier I dreamt always of Spain and Europe. Some things are very difficult in my country. People have closed minds.'

I realized in that moment that Zine had not come to Spain because he needed the money. Money in order to survive on an everyday level, perhaps, but he wasn't an unemployed farmer desperate to keep his family going with no chance of work back home, as was the case with so many immigrants. His coming here was more from an emotional need – escaping a world he felt restricted him.

He sipped on his coffee, creamy foam sticking to the week's growth of whiskers on his top lip. He wiped it away, soil from the farm still lodged under his fingernails.

'The Rifian told me a story – about a musician who went to see a doctor. The musician was suffering from all kinds of complaints, saying his arms and legs hurt, and he was unhappy. So the doctor said: "It's true that you haven't performed your latest composition in public yet, isn't it?" And the musician nodded. "Then perhaps you would play it for me now," said the doctor. So the musician pulled out his oud and started to play, and when he finished the doctor asked him to play it again, and then again, several times over. Then the doctor asked the musician to stand up. "You are cured now," he said. "What you had inside was affecting your outside. But now it has been released, and you are better." And it was true – the musician was totally cured.

'You see,' he continued as I thought a minute about the story, 'I always wanted to escape, to get away from Morocco. It was inside me, like the musician. I couldn't think of anything else. But just one change and . . .'

As he was talking I was reminded of my father. Having lived in America and the south of England most of his life, he'd returned to his home county of Lancashire when he retired. The rest of the family had raised an eyebrow when he'd told us he was moving back, but ever since I'd noticed a certain centredness about him, as though living in the countryside of his birth, with its hills and brooks, connected him with . . . what was it? Roots? I wasn't sure. I envied him in some ways – to feel that somewhere there was a place you belonged. Unable to say where I came from, I'd thought for a while that I'd found something similar here in Spain.

Zine sighed heavily. 'I want to come back to Valencia, Jasie.' The smoke from his cigarette crept up the woollen sleeve of his jumper. 'I want to be with Lucía.'

We stepped back outside into the fog, thicker now, and wet, bearing the promise of cold merciless winter. The beat of the marchers' drum thudded relentlessly, softened slightly by the microscopic droplets of water that padded the air. The demonstrators weaved ghost-like through the square, barely visible now, short bursts of enthusiasm given to their anti-war cry as they began to tire and think of going home for lunch.

They used to tell a legend about Toledo, and the old Tower of Hercules that had once stood here in pre-Moorish days:

An ancient king wished to hide away a secret, and so he built the tower and locked the secret inside. Before he died he ordered that every king after him should add a new lock and bolt to the door so that

247

nobody could ever find out what the secret was. Twenty-six kings followed him and carried out his wish, until one day a weak and petulant man ascended the throne. Against the advice of all his ministers, the new king had the tower door smashed open. Inside he found a round room with a gold and silver table placed in the centre. On it he read 'This is the table of David, son of Solomon, peace be upon him.' On the table stood an urn. With one swoop, the king knocked it to the ground, breaking it into a thousand pieces. Inside there was a parchment, which said: 'Whenever this tower is violated and this urn broken, the people painted on the walls of this room will invade Spain, overthrow its kings and subdue the entire land.' The king looked up at the walls in horror and saw bearded horsemen wearing white and black turbans on their heads, carrying curved scimitars in their hands, poised for deadly attack. The year was 710 and the king's name was Roderic, the last of the Visigothic kings. Twelve months later he was dead, his kingdom conquered, Islamic armies having swept him aside. It was the beginning of Al-Andalus.

As I watched the protesters now, their eyes filled with fear, with a kind of millenarian dread of the consequences of the coming war, there was a momentary echo in my mind of the Twin Towers in New York and crazed suicide squads killing people in a frenzy of hate. There was a strong sense that we were at another turning point, the beginning of another chapter in the long, complex and often violent relationship between the Islamic and Western worlds. Would they be telling similar legends about the World Trade Center in another thousand years' time?

We crossed the square and went looking for somewhere to eat. I thought Zine might enjoy some typical and decidedly un-Muslim roast suckling pig, so tender you were supposed to be able to cut it into pieces using the sides of two plates. It was a delicacy in Christianized central Spain, a potent symbol of religious ownership of the land, which over the centuries had turned into an innocent culinary speciality: a bit like eating hamburgers in countries which today feel the influence of American culture and might. They weren't so interested in what the Moors had to offer in Toledo any more, except in terms of tourist revenue as, museum-like, the city showcased its more illustrious past. Craftsmen still produced damascene metalwork – first developed, as its name implied, in Damascus – but these days the black and gold design work was as likely to decorate the scabbard of a Japanese sword in the window of a souvenir shop, or a 'genuine' medieval-style pole-axe. The period of translations had eventually come to an end as the whole tone of relations between the different faiths began to change: pogroms against the Jews were whipped up by St Vincent Ferrer in the fourteenth century, the Inquisition took hold in the fifteenth and beyond, and finally the Jews and Moriscos were expelled. Periods of tolerance and understanding, it seemed, came to an end, often a violent one: blips of humanity, before falling back into impoverished barbarism.

'From the beginning of the Renaissance, Arab art ceased to be popular,' Titus Burckhardt had written of Spain. 'Above all, there no longer existed the spiritual link between the different religious communities. In the Middle Ages, Christians, Jews and Muslims had inhabited the same spiritual space, for all that their respective creeds varied. This world ceased to exist for the culture of the Renaissance.'

As we passed through the demonstration, a middle-aged man handed us a leaflet. 'No War in Iraq,' it shouted. 'Stop the Oil War.'

Zine and I headed away from the square and down the narrow stony streets of the ancient city. The smell of roasting meats issuing from shadowy restaurants was making my empty stomach do somersaults.

'No more farm work, then,' I said.

He was silent for a minute, and I wondered if he was ignoring me, or hadn't heard.

'I love Lucía,' he said eventually.

MONTSERRAT

*T*he rich, forested hills of Catalonia stretched far into the distance as the tooth-like range of Montserrat – the sawn-off mountain – loomed over us in the clearing air. Yellowing oak woods like the fur on an old teddy bear surrounded us, with rivers and waterfalls pushing out of mountainsides like white handkerchiefs. The brilliant sunlight created a chequerboard effect of shade and light at the corner of my eye as we drove past powerful trees.

From further away the mountain resembled a business chart on an executive's office wall, but closer up the grey peaks of this bizarre hill reminded me of the great bony fingers of some of Dalí's paintings with their broken half-human forms. The spiritual heart of Catalonia, this was the second holiest place in Christian Spain after Santiago de Compostela, and the church and monastery that had been built into the side of this mountain had been the only place Franco had allowed the celebration of mass in Catalan. It was also home to La Moreneta – the most famous of Spain's mysterious Black Madonnas.

Catalonia was one last area of Spain I wanted to

explore before heading back to Valencia. The Catalan-speaking state of Andorra might have a name derived from the Arabic *al-ghandura* – the fallen woman – but on the face of it this far north-eastern corner of Spain, on the border with France, had little of Al-Andalus about it. For centuries it had been a border region between Moors and Christians but, ordered and European, it felt a world away from the south and its daily reminders of North Africa. Yet I had an intuition that here, as much as anywhere in Spain, more gems were waiting to be discovered. Zine, back in the passenger seat, would have to wait a couple more days to be reunited with Lucía.

'This is an angry place,' he said when we arrived at the monastery. 'People here look angry.'

It was a Saturday afternoon, and a number of wedding parties were flowing in and out of the basilica in a blur of white veils and taffeta, towards the restaurants and supermarkets that surrounded it. How many of them knew that the material for their dresses had first been brought from the Middle East and that the word was a straight copy from the Arabic *tafta*, I wondered.

Zine was smoking his L&M cigarettes, smoke curling away in the wind down into the wet, rainy valley below, dark clouds climbing rapidly towards us up the thickly wooded mountainside.

'I've never been to a church,' he said.

I took him by the elbow and led him to the entrance.

'Will they let me in? As a . . . ?'

'Don't worry,' I said.

He gave a half-smile, not quite convinced, but I steered him over the threshold before he could ask any questions.

Inside the church was dark and layered thick with gilt Baroque design work. Gold-painted geometrical and vegetal motifs decorated the walls, columns and arches painted in heavy blues and greens. I walked down the central aisle of the nave as Zine headed off to hide in the shadows. Towards the front, a small group of elderly arthritic women were doing their best to kneel down and pray, spotlights focused on the golden altar and the Black Madonna sitting high up with Baby Jesus on her lap. The place was quiet and still; not a sound was made by the dozen or so visitors pacing the stone slabs of the floor.

'Hey, you!' In an instant, the sanctified atmosphere broke as a hysterical male voice echoed suddenly around the ancient stonework. Everyone in the church quickly turned round to see what was happening. It was amazing how fast some of those old women could move when distracted from their prayers. I looked around for Zine.

'Thief!' The voice shouted again, coming from the direction of the altar. I turned to see a priest shouting at a young man whose back was turned to me. I couldn't see his face, but knew at once who it was.

The priest's eyes were screwed tight like whirlwinds, his cheeks flushed red with anger, his hands outstretched as though about to grasp Zine's neck.

'¡No se toca la Cruz! You don't touch the Cross!'

I ran up quickly and pulled Zine away. The priest looked like the kind who don't mind having the odd scrap every now and again.

'It's his first time in a church,' I said, trying to explain, placing myself between them as best I could.

'¡Fuera de aquí! Get out!' he shouted. Foam-like spit bubbled at the corner of his mouth.

'He's no thief. He was just curious.'

'OUT!'

Zine had already backed away almost to the door; it was clear this man of God was not prepared to discuss things. I couldn't help wondering if he'd worked as a bouncer before deciding to devote his life to Christ.

I was reluctant to give in to this blatantly aggressive approach, especially in a church, especially when the accusation was false, but the priest lunged at me threateningly, to make the point that I was taking too long to leave.

The old women glared as I walked to the doorway out of which Zine had already passed, while the priest muttered behind my back.

Zine was sitting on the stone steps in the sun-blanched courtyard outside the basilica, a white look of fear on his face. He scratched around his ears nervously.

'I didn't even touch the cross,' he said, staring at the stone floor.

'They probably thought you wanted to be converted,' I said, sitting down next to him. I was furious at the priest, but thought making light of it might help to calm Zine down.

He stood up sharply, though, and walked off without a word, pacing quickly and heavily through the black shade of the protecting arcade into the open square. I watched him disappear, and remained where I was: better to leave him alone for a while.

Violent priests. I breathed deeply in an attempt to calm my rage. Unfortunately it was not the first time I'd been threatened in a church: a priest had once attacked me in Assisi for no good reason, grabbing me by the scruff of the neck and throwing me out. Yet still

255

I was shocked by it. Wrongly, perhaps: the image these frock-wearers gave was one of peace and harmony, yet you only had to look at their faces for a few minutes to realize the majority of them were semi-detached frustrated balls of anger. In fact it was surprising they didn't have a go more often. I just wished that Zine's first experience in a church hadn't been quite so dramatic.

I waited for a while, but after twenty minutes I realized he wasn't coming back, and walked carefully into the basilica again through the special side entrance designed for visits to the Black Madonna. The passageway led you past the chapels on the right-hand side, so I couldn't be seen by the worshippers in the church itself. There was no sign of the priest.

I climbed an ornate staircase round the back of the altar until I was standing some ten or fifteen feet up, where the statue was encased in heavy silverwork, with thick bas-reliefs on either side depicting biblical scenes. The Madonna herself looked as though she belonged to a very different age to the one that had wrapped her in this ornate splendour. She was draped in golden robes and with a gold crown, her head out of proportion to her slim, elegant body, and her face long and stylized: a sharp, almost unnatural nose turned up slightly; a receding chin; low forehead and narrow eyes. And this strangeness about her was accentuated by her being as black as night, as her face and hands were made of what looked like ebony. In her right hand she held a black ball that visitors were supposed to kiss, and on her left sat the Baby Jesus, as black as his mother, but without her other-worldliness – more cherub-like, with golden curly locks flowing down either side of his black cheeks.

The Madonna was said to be a work of Romanesque sculpture from the twelfth century, but many preferred the legend that she was the work of St Luke, brought to Catalonia by St Peter and hidden during the Moorish conquest, only to be lost and then rediscovered by seven shepherds tending their herds one evening on Montserrat. Whatever her origin, there was something arresting about the statue, her far-away look reminiscent of the famous bust of Nefertiti in Berlin. Perhaps it was true that Black Madonnas were a remnant of the Egyptian cult of Isis and the baby Horus. Yet there were other theories about the origins of this strange cult: Robert Graves had suggested she represented the Black Goddess, a wiser version of the poetic muse, the White Goddess. Certainly there seemed to be few pointers within Christianity itself. Mary, either black or white, was barely mentioned in the Bible at all – just a handful of references in the Gospels and one line in the Acts of the Apostles. The Qur'an, on the other hand, devoted a whole *sura*, or chapter, to her, as the mother of one of the prophets recognized by Islam – Jesus. Was it only coincidence that the cult of the Virgin Mary was more intense in parts of Europe that had felt the greatest Muslim influence in the Middle Ages, namely Spain, southern Italy and southern France? Walking into some of the churches in these countries you might easily think Christianity was a goddess-based religion, so dominant were the images of her. In the past I might have thought it a bizarre idea, that Catholicism might have been inspired by Islam in such a way. Yet as I'd travelled around I'd come across so many instances of subtle crossovers between these two religions that now the idea seemed more than possible. Black was a significant colour for Muslims: the colour of wisdom. There might well be another connection there with the Black Madonnas. Gazing at the statue for some time, though, I could find no other clues. It was a question that, at least for now, would have to remain unresolved.

Zine was waiting for me outside, a book in his hand. He held it out to me as I walked up to him.

'I've found something for you,' he said.

'Are you all right?'

'Look at it,' he insisted.

It was a small, colourful children's book with a drawing on the front of two men sitting on a hilltop dressed in Arab costume. *Els Gegants*, it said in Catalan – The Giants. It looked familiar for some reason, and glancing at the spine I realized it was from the same publisher as the book of Musa the Moor that Chimo had sold me back in Valencia.

'I saw the picture of the man in a fez and thought you'd be interested in it,' Zine said. He'd bought it for me, despite having almost no money.

We sat down on the steps leading away from the church and, curious, I began to read the story out loud:

It was said that when the Moors had conquered Catalonia they were helped by very tall, ferocious giants. But as time went on the giants got used to the good life, and when the Christians were about to retake the area, and the Moors were leaving in droves, the giants, now quiet and peace-loving, decided to stay. At a special meeting they all decided they would ask for help from the witch Hipolita, who lived near by. And so in the darkness of her cave she brewed them a special potion made from secret ingredients. Flying off on her broom to where the giants lived, she pronounced the magic words *Abelú, Quemira, Bossanal*, and sprinkled the potion on their hands. All at once torrential rain began to fall, thunder bellowed out and forked lightning split the sky. The giants were terrified. But no sooner had they realized what was happening than they all turned into stone, frozen solid in the form of the mysterious and enigmatic mountain now known as Montserrat. And so they slept for years and years until . . . One day Gertrudis, the only daughter of the Count of Barcelona, fell mysteriously ill. Feeling sad and listless, she spent all day lying in bed, neither eating nor sleeping. Fearing for his daughter's life, the Count called all the doctors of the land to try and cure her, but none could help the poor girl. Then one day, a young troubadour arrived. Convinced of the healing power of music, he stood below Gertrudis' bedroom window and began playing the most beautiful music you could ever imagine. Days passed, and the days turned into weeks, and months and even years, and still the troubadour played until one day the Count's daughter, her curiosity finally aroused, got up to see who was playing such sweet music. But having lain down for so long, she only got as far as putting her nose out of the window before she had to return to bed. The next day she tried again, and this time she managed to get as far as feeling the sun on her face before she had to lie down once more. But on the third day, the troubadour's music now having healed her completely, she was able to lean out of the window and see for the first time who had been playing for her all this time. And as is the way in these things, as soon as the couple set eyes on each other they fell in love and decided to get married. The Count was deliriously

259

happy when he found out his daughter was cured, and decided the wedding should take place on Montserrat. Over three hundred musicians, troubadours, jugglers, acrobats and harlequins came to put on a spectacle in the square in front of the church. The noise they made was so great, and echoed so loudly around the mountain, that the rocks began to wake up, and remember the life they had lived so many years before, breaking out from their stony shapes to become . . . giants once more. And moved by the music and the drums and crashing cymbals, they began to dance with the wedding guests, spinning and spinning around in circles. And when the party was over, and the music finally stopped, they returned to stone and the mountain took on its peculiar shape once more. And since that day they say the giants only come alive again to dance when sons and daughters of the Counts of Barcelona get married in the church of Montserrat.

The holy mountain of Catalonia, one of the most important Christian sites in the whole of Spain, was in fact the resting place of Moorish giants. I laughed. Peel back a layer or two and the Arab past was clearly there, like a veiled dancing girl.

'See?' Zine said.

'What?'

'They can't get rid of us Moors that easily.'

I punched him in the ribs: he was stealing my lines.

BARCELONA

*H*is Royal Highness Prince José-María de Almuzara of the Banu Qasi, Grand Master of the Order of Muza, Pasha of Islam, Honorary General of Italy, Grand Marshal of the Sovereign and Military Order of the Temple of Jerusalem, Secret Counsellor of the Ancient Byzantine Catholic and Apostolic Church, and President of the Catalan section of the Asociación Española de Orientalistas, granted me an audience in his small flat just off the Diagonal avenue. Thanks to a contact from Pedro, I had been given the chance to meet the last male member of a family that had once reigned over a third of Spain during Islamic times: a short man with liver spots and badly dyed black hair showing its natural white beneath a shower of dandruff. He had a certain presence, though, and was self-assured, as though conscious of his royal lineage and proud of it.

'I feel this Moorishness in my blood,' he said as we sat down on a painted wooden bench-like sofa, 'even if I don't know anything about my family's past; it's inside me.'

It was everywhere around him as well. The flat was

in a small district near the centre of Barcelona, built perhaps a hundred years before, where the buildings were either one or two storeys high – the kind of flat, low effect you get on cowboy filmsets. Inside, though, was like walking into a tourist shop in the Khan el-Khalili bazaar in Cairo. Brightly coloured leather pouffes with gold design work were strewn on the floor; lacquer-work tables with mind-boggling Arabesque patterns leant against the walls; Arab-style damascene steel swords such as I'd seen in Toledo, inlaid with the motto of the Nasrid dynasty of Granada – *wa la ghaliba illa Allah*, no conqueror but God – decorated the walls; while brass Moroccan lanterns with coloured glass hung from the ceiling. Most had been bought on various trips to the Middle East with the prince's friend Guillermo, an elderly man who shadowed us as we walked around the flat.

The prince pointed to a giant golden urn standing in a corner.

'The shah of Iran ordered several hundred of those from a man here in Barcelona, because there was no one else in the world who could make them. I knew the craftsman and he gave me one of the spares.'

I looked down at the enormous lump of gold-coloured metal next to me.

'Try lifting it; it's incredibly heavy!'

After a token effort I pleaded back problems and gave up.

The tour of the small living space continued, passing through Ali Baba archways and treading on Oriental rugs. The prince had had a shield made with the family emblem blazoned on the front – a gold octagon on a green background. He'd had a ring made in similar fashion, with gold, diamonds and emerald, and it jutted out from the third finger on his left hand.

'My family were rulers of this part of Spain even in Visigothic times and before – in the Iberian period,' he said. 'It was called the Cassi tribe then. Some of them colonized Britain and ended up in the Oxford area. In Roman times the family name became Cassius, then Banu Qasi in Arabic – the tribe of Qasi: that's the name we took after the Moorish invasion.'

A play on words came to mind: combining the Arabic and Spanish, the family name translated into something like the McAlmosts. It could hardly have been more apt.

The family story was a common one throughout the territories conquered by Muslim armies, where agreements were often reached with existing local rulers rather than changes being imposed. In what was now Aragón and Catalonia, Prince José-María's family, the Banu Qasi, had stayed in power by converting to Islam at the time of the Moorish conquest. The head of the family accompanied the victorious Muslim armies back to Damascus to be presented before the caliph, and his son married the daughter of the Moorish ruler – Musa. The child resulting from this marriage took the name of his maternal grandfather and henceforth it became a family name, later transforming into the present surname Almuzara: the prince was therefore a direct descendant of Musa the Moor, the man whose secret treasure I'd been trying to find.

In the years after the Moorish conquest, a policy of marrying into the most powerful families on both the Christian and Muslim sides ensured that the Banu Qasi remained the most powerful group in the north-east of the country, and were even dubbed 'the third kings of Spain' – after the Muslim emir in the south and the Christian king in the north.

'We had castles all over this area – right up to Huesca and beyond,' the prince said. 'Both Abd al-Rahman III and the Bourbon kings are descendants of the Banu Qasi.'

Abd al-Rahman III, the red-haired, blue-eyed caliph of Córdoba, had ruled over the Golden Age of Al-Andalus; the Bourbons were not only erstwhile kings of France, but were now occupying the throne of modern Spain.

'Some time in the sixties the Ministry of Justice decided to sort out all the claims that were about at that time; there was one man who even said he was the descendant of Montezuma! So they came here and spent – what was it? Three weeks here? No, two months – looking at the papers I've got – over 2,000 pieces of paper to prove my lineage. Look, even Pope John XXIII recognized me.'

We walked over to a framed document showing the jowl-faced patriarch with his abnormally large ears.

'I've got more titles than I can remember. Here, some of them are on the back of my card. But there are more. I've got them written down somewhere.'

I was more interested, though, in what this man represented of the Islamic past, perhaps a living gem from Musa's treasure: an embodiment of both the Islamic and Christian elements that fused in Spain to make it the unique country it was. What did he feel? Moorish? Spanish?

'I'm Catalan,' he said. 'Then Spanish, then Moorish. The Arabs were here for a thousand years. A thousand years!' He raised his finger. 'The Romans only controlled Spain for three or four centuries, the Visigoths less. People just don't remember that.'

I decided to ask the prince about his views on Muslims currently living in Spain. What did he think of the proposal to build a mosque in Premiá?

At this point Guillermo, who had been sitting quietly until that moment, exploded.

'It's a scandal!' he screamed.

I looked round. The man had barely moved since we sat down, perched elegantly in his smart grey suit, his grey hair beautifully groomed. His features were Germanic and he had light-coloured eyes. I'd assumed that, as a friend of the Arab-loving prince, and his companion on numerous trinket-buying trips to the Middle East, he would be better disposed to the small Muslim community in the coastal town who, after buying a plot of land in the centre, were now being denied permission by the Catalan authorities to build a mosque there.

'They make too much noise,' he said. 'There's nowhere to park, the streets are narrow and they come and take all the parking spaces and people can't sleep at night because of the wailing of the muezzin.'

I was surprised. This was Spain, the noisiest country in Europe. And there was *never* anywhere to park, but you always managed to squeeze in somewhere nonetheless – on the pavement, double-parked, on the zebra crossing or simply in the middle of the road, as long as people could still get past. But Guillermo was steaming.

'We can't have a mosque in the centre of the town. They all work in the fields anyway. They should build it on the industrial estate so they don't bother anyone.'

I felt uneasy with this kind of talk. The Premiá story had been one of many over recent months that high-lighted the growing importance of the immigration issue in Spain, and you felt an increasing tension as riots or racially motivated murders were reported in the news. The country's birth rate was falling dramatically and was now the lowest in Europe. Within a couple of decades demographers were predicting the population would fall from forty million to thirty million. Immigration would have to be one of the solutions, yet Spain, as I'd learnt, had a fundamental and historical problem with the people closest at hand to fill the gap – the *moros*. Officially there were well over 200,000 Moroccans in the country – more than twice as many as the second-largest group, Ecuadoreans. The authorities were bending over backwards to keep them out, though, trying to open the door at the same time to more 'acceptable' immigrants such as Spanish-speaking Latin Americans or Christians from Eastern Europe. A similar policy had been adopted during the Reconquest, when German, French and other northern settlers had been invited over to farm lands newly conquered from the Moors. The legacy of those times was still as strong as ever.

I was puzzled that the prince's friend should take such an aggressive attitude towards Muslim immigrants.

'They wouldn't bother anyone.' The prince interrupted Guillermo with a smile. 'The town hall gave them permission. Everything was all right until the Catalan authorities got involved.'

Guillermo sniffed and looked about to embark on a new anti-Islamic attack. I felt the meeting was going off the rails.

'What about religion, though,' I asked the prince quickly. 'Are you Christian, Muslim . . . ?'

'Neither and both,' he said. 'Islam and Christianity are essentially the same. I don't like to use the word "God". I think if anything of that nature exists it is too far beyond human experience to even give it a name. One cannot know God rationally. Perhaps only intuitively, and then only as cells in the body might know the thoughts of the brain. They can send messages – prayers, if you like – to the brain and the brain can choose to respond or not, by scratching an itch, for example. But that is all.'

There was a pause for a moment as I let this sink in. The tone of the conversation had changed rather suddenly after Guillermo's outburst.

'You're a Pasha of Islam, but also recognized by the Pope.'

'I'm recognized all over Europe. I have titles from all kinds of countries. Guillermo, do you know where the list is?'

Guillermo looked sulky. 'They're written down somewhere,' he said finally. He seemed like a child, annoyed at not being the centre of attention.

But the prince returned to the subject of his family, and had me read aloud long passages from a self-published book supporting his claim to the illustrious Banu Qasi lineage.

''Abd Allah ibn Muhammad ibn Llop was succeeded by . . .'

'Yes, this bit, this bit,' he said, wriggling in his chair enthusiastically.

'What happened to your family during the Reconquest?' I asked, trying to change the subject.

'Some went into hiding in the Huesca region. We had castles stretching all the way from the Pyrenees to the sea.'

This great territory – almost a kingdom in itself, with castles and villages and houses – which the family had held on to through Iberian, Roman, Visigothic and Moorish times, had been lost as the Christians pushed south. Now there was just a little flat, decorated with nick-nacks from a North African bazaar.

I flicked forwards a few pages in the book and found a reference to the Order of Muza, of which the prince was Grand Master.

'A noble and gentlemanly order, without any political bias, that works to bring about the union of religions and the brotherhood of the Arab peoples with the West.' One of its ranks was the 'Great Star of Islam', which carried the title 'Sidi', as in El Cid.

We drank ice-cold Cava from silver goblets, with a toast to the house of the Banu Qasi, before finally it was time for me to leave. Exchanging cards, we shook hands. It was as though everything moved around him, but the prince was always still.

'He's got women crowding around him all the time but he's never interested,' Guillermo said with a cheeky smile. 'I've got a new girlfriend . . .'

'No heir, then?' I asked the prince. He shook his head. It appeared to be a sore point.

'Come and call when you're next in Barcelona,' he said as I walked down the stairs to the front door.

Guillermo and I walked out into the white evening light.

'The town hall is going to pull his house down,' he said. 'They want to build more towers like those.' We looked up at the glass and concrete office blocks stretching up from the next street. 'Damn them.'

'They're throwing the prince out of his own house?'

'He'll be all right.'

269

And with that he was gone; the Vizier of the Order of Muza, hurrying round the corner to catch a bus home.

Not only a living remnant of the Moors, I thought. So much about the prince embodied Spain's relationship with its Islamic past: partial understanding, hidden in a corner somewhere like an exotic but slightly embarrassing piece of furniture. And when it didn't suit or it got in the way, a simple rejection or wiping clean. Just like the city of Barcelona was doing now with the prince himself, the last of the McAlmosts.

I met up with Zine at a bar on the edge of the Ramblas, the central avenue that ran like a spinal cord through the city from the Plaça de Catalunya down to the sea and the statue of Columbus pointing out, bizarrely, towards the east. Another little-known Moorish legacy, 'Rambla' came from *ramla* in Arabic, meaning sand, or a sandy stretch of river bed where a river flows into the sea. Alicante had a similar avenue – La Rambla – pointing down to the harbour, while in Alexandria I remembered catching trams to Ramleh, the main square by the Esplanade where we'd suicidally buy 'death burgers' for lunch from Abdessalem's rancid little fast-food stall near the taxi rank.

As I sipped an orange juice, I looked at the people sitting around us at the bar, and took note of what they were eating and drinking, their clothes, what they were doing: one middle-aged man sat at the table next to us wearing cotton trousers and a silk shirt, sucking his lips and gums as though he had just cleaned his teeth; at another table a couple were eating meatballs in thick onion and tomato sauce with rice and a spinach salad; another man, black hair slicked back in the fashion of many right-wing Spaniards, read a front-page newspaper story about the latest rocket technology about to be used against the Iraqis. He seemed uninterested, though, and turned to the horoscopes, sipping on an iced soft drink in a tall glass. Just a few feet away two elderly men were leaning over their chess game, one of them absent-mindedly stirring the sugar into his coffee with a continuous *tink-tink-tink* as he tried to work out his next move. Three women on the other side were chatting incessantly, but for a second their conversation inexplicably dried up.

'Must be an angel passing overhead,' one said.

And I began to see. Perhaps because of my visit to the prince, or as a result of my journey, as I took in my surroundings connections began to form in my mind: the picture I had been trying to grasp for so long. Before it had seemed like something just outside my field of vision. But now I realized that so much of this scene, in modern Barcelona, came directly from the Moors. Yet the connection was almost invisible.

I wondered if the man wearing cotton trousers knew that cotton was first grown on a large scale by the Moors in Spain, from where it passed to Europe. The word 'cotton' – *algodón* in Spanish – came from the Arabic *al-qutun*. Silk-making knowledge was brought into the Arab world after 840 when the astrologer-poet Yahya al-Ghazal, or John the Gazelle, visited Byzantium. He smuggled the techniques back with him to Spain, from where silk-making began to travel north. Toothpaste arrived in Spain from Baghdad in the ninth century; meatballs, rice and spinach all came to Spain via the Moors; the paper the newspaper was printed on was a direct legacy of Europe's first paper mill at Játiva; rocket technology was built on the higher mathematics translated into Latin from Arabic in Toledo; horoscopes, astrology, and with it astronomy, were brought to Europe through Moorish Spain – today astronomers still refer to many stars using their original Arab names, for example 'Betelgeuse'.

Iced soft drinks were mentioned in the *Thousand and One Nights*, where they were served to the Caliph Harun al-Rashid – the Arabic word for iced drinks, *sharba*, was still remembered in the Spanish word *sorbete* and the English 'sherbet' and 'sorbet', as well as 'syrup'. The first European to discover the formula to make glass was an Andalusi Spaniard in the ninth century called Ibn Firnas – Moorish Spain subsequently became a producer of glass and exported it to its Christian neighbours. Ziryab, the musician trendsetter from Baghdad, first brought chess to Spain in the ninth century. Around the same time, a host of Persian superstitions gained currency in Islamic Spain, subsequently making their way into Europe – among them were the ideas that angels passing overhead stopped conversations in mid-flow, that breaking mirrors was generally a bad thing, and that the number thirteen was unlucky. Moorish Spain had also introduced sugar to Europe – sugar was mentioned in Spain as early as 714, just three years after the Moorish invasion, and sugar cane became one of the staple crops on the Iberian peninsula. Oranges were virtually unknown in Europe before the Arab conquest.

I saw all this in a single, compacted second, like a dot of concentrated energy.

Ask anyone and they would say Spain was symbolized by bullfighting and flamenco, perhaps also the Civil War. 'Moorish' Spain was a detail of that picture, limited to the south of the country at most.

I understood in that moment, however, that it was the very canvas on which the country had been painted, sometimes obscured by the image represented, visible only at the fringes, but always there, just a layer or two underneath. And if you looked closely you could see it in the texture behind the paint, and very occasionally where the artist had left the canvas bare.

Ordering some snails in tomato sauce, I told Zine about my meeting with Prince Almuzara.

'Sounds like you found Musa himself,' he said when I'd finished.

CYBER MARY

'¡*Qué fuerte, tío!* Bloody hell!'

The semi-naked muscle man bellowed his catch-phrase for the hundredth time as a blonde topless Mother Christmas handed him the butt of the joint that had already circled the cramped room.

'My nipples are itching,' she said. 'I think it's this gold body paint.'

'Here, I've got some soothing cream.'

A second topless dancer – a redhead – handed her a crumpled tube as she scratched at the stretched aureole around her pneumatic breasts, peering downwards with a frown that made the ligaments stand out in her neck. Her fingernails left ugly tracks in her skin.

'I'll have to make up again,' she said. 'You can see the scar.'

'Should I give her a hand?' Zine whispered to me, fake beard wobbling loosely on his chin when he spoke.

'I heard that!' The rest of the dressing room laughed as she turned her slender back on us to make herself up again.

I said nothing: they were just working, like the rest

of us that night. Some taken on for their dancing, others just for the way they looked, like Zine himself.

'*Un moro* as Joseph?' Ramón had whined when I'd mentioned my Moroccan friend. One of the dancers had pulled out and he needed a last-minute replacement to play the putative father of God at the disco. '*Ostias, tío.* That's perfect. Is he good looking?' And he'd giggled over the phone like a schoolgirl.

'He's got a girlfriend, and she's pregnant.'

'*Ah, bueno.* I'll just look, then.'

A friend had recommended drinking diet cola to ward off the worst symptoms of nausea, but two months after we'd got back to Valencia Lucía was still suffering as the first signs of the half-Moorish child growing inside her began to show. Despite spending most of the morning lying down in a pale dizzy haze, squeezing her rehearsals into the afternoons and performing occasionally at night, she was the happiest I had ever known her, her full face fixed into a wide grin.

'*¡Qué feliz me has hecho!*' she sang. '*¡Ay qué bien! Me lo has devuelto.*'

She'd been overjoyed when I brought Zine back with me; any sourness that had accompanied his previous departure had evaporated. Well rounded as she was, she seemed to have lost quite a bit of weight when I first saw her on our return.

'She thought she was never going to see him again,' Salud told me. 'Zine had been on the point of staying behind with her when you left, but she told him to go. She was worried about him not finding work.'

I understood why he'd said so little about the separation now. In the end I had probably been holding him more to my promise than he had.

Their reconciliation was immediate: Zine asked to be dropped off directly at her flat when we finally arrived back in the city, and when he still hadn't shown up at our place by the following morning I assumed the best.

'I've told her everything,' he confided in me when he called a couple of days later. 'She says she wants me to stay this time, Jasie!'

He'd moved in with her, but they didn't find out till a couple of weeks later that she was already over a month pregnant from when he'd previously been in Valencia. After just a week of honeymooning, he'd been spending most of the day out of the house trying to make contacts in the building trade or among other Moroccans who might be able to help him find a job.

'Just get married,' I said when he told me the news about the baby. 'That would sort out the legal stuff, at least.'

'I want to find work myself first,' he said.

Marriage at this stage would mean he'd failed: a lift up to the top when what he wanted was to have climbed there himself. He had chosen to come back to Valencia to be with Lucía, but at the same time I could understand how he might want to feel settled as a result of his own efforts. I was concerned, though, that this was not the only reason for his reluctance to get married – I wasn't convinced it was a path he was ready to go down yet. Impending fatherhood had been invigorating but had also beaten something out of him.

'I want you to be my Arabic teacher,' I said, trying to find ways to keep him going financially. 'Formally. I've lost so much of it since university. You can teach me Moroccan dialect. I'll pay.'

'No, Jasie. I can find someone else for you, though.'

And so it had gone on.

'I'm going to be the father of a half-Spanish child,' he said one morning when we met at the bar on the corner of my street. He gripped the table, coffee swirling inside our cups, before falling back into his chair with a sigh. 'But what kind of father am I going to be? Lucía's family give her money, but I need to be as welcome here as my child will be. Not the sponging immigrant, not the crazy *moro*.'

His thoughts and feelings at that moment were not dissimilar to some of my own. There were different rules abroad. The question was whether it liberated you or imprisoned you even more. The line between the two wasn't always clear.

Yet he seemed happy with Lucía. The two of them were out most nights going to gigs or just hanging out in the bars of the Carmen district, Zine sliding into her life like a missing piece of a jigsaw puzzle: she knew lots of people in the city from her performances and had a circle of friends who almost always went out together. If anything, I thought it too set up for him: the flat, the social life. The pregnancy had been the only mistake in it all, but now they both seemed pleased about it. Lucía was already turning down gigs for the following summer. '*Voy a ser madre*,' she'd say, a calm serenity filling her young round face. Just a girl, but she was growing into the idea of motherhood just as the baby grew inside her.

'Can you see me filling out?' And she'd place her hands on her chest. '*Mira, por fin tengo tetas de verdad.*'

The pressure Zine placed on himself to get work without any help – even from Lucía – was increasing. With the holidays starting, he had found nothing apart from the odd day of work, cash in hand. So when Ramón told me he needed someone last minute for the Christmas Eve disco job, I immediately put his name forward. Ramón accepted without any hesitation: in the upside-down world of the *gente de la noche*, where appearance was substance, the Moroccan would be exotic and exciting.

Zine, though, had little idea about what to expect. Valencian discos – great warehouses on the edge of the city – were surreal places. Salud had been working in them sporadically for years – it was a way of earning quick money when there was no work acting or dancing flamenco – and recently I'd been joining her: as a hired driver, or even, like tonight, as part of the performance. Neither of us, though, were of the 'tribe' – people looking for an image that involved dressing like clowns and taking large amounts of *pastillas*. I wasn't sure what they put in the drugs these days, but there was an increasingly hard-edged quality to disco environments. Not the love-in of Ecstasy days: it felt angrier and sharper.

'It's a hundred and twenty euros for just a night's work,' I said.

'Do I have to dance?' Zine looked doubtful.

'Not really. We just get dressed up and look decorative.'

'I'm not sure.'

'It's fine,' I said. 'If anything, it's boring. We sit around in the dressing room most of the night, then three or four times we go out and walk about.'

'What?'

'It's Christmas Eve. They just want us as a sort of walking nativity scene. You know, the thing with the Baby Jesus . . .'

'Yes, I know. The cows and all that. What are you doing?'

'Salud's going as Mary. And I'm ... I'm the shepherd,' I said, raising an eyebrow. 'Don't laugh.'

He smiled. 'So who am I, then?'

'You'll be Joseph.'

'Me? Ha! Imagine that – a Moroccan as the father of Jesus.'

And there we all were, cramped in a huddle at three a.m. on Christmas morning, the most bizarre nativity scene I'd ever seen, waiting to be called out for our second appearance, trying not to doze off as the heavy bass *oomba oomba* of the music below shook the walls and sent us into varying trance-like states.

'*Ay*, it keeps smearing.' Chelo, the blonde Mother Christmas, turned back to face the room, gold paint all over her fingers and more lines criss-crossing her breasts where she'd tried to repair the make-up.

'*Qué fuerte, tío.*'

In most cases it was hard to see where the knife had gone in and the silicon inserted, but Chelo, who when not dancing half-naked was a soldier in the Spanish army, had been unlucky – ugly jagged lines disfigured her triple-D cups and she'd lost almost all sensation. 'Guys love 'em but they don't do much for me,' she'd once told Salud. I wondered how anyone with such large appendages had ever got into the armed forces in the first place. Didn't they get in the way when firing a rifle? What about crawling on the ground to avoid enemy fire? This girl would bounce three feet in the air. Perhaps they used her as a decoy.

'Fancy a drink, Princess?' Alberto, the dwarf Santa, was playing barman, handing out whisky and Cokes and Tía Marías from the box of booze he'd found

281

hidden behind the metal filing cabinet. It helped pass the time between performances, as all seven of us tried to squeeze into the purple and black painted store cupboard that had been designated our changing room for the night.

'Bastards wanted me to come as the Baby Jesus,' Alberto explained as he filled my plastic tumbler. 'Dressed in a nappy with a dummy in my mouth. Fuck that. Took me three hours to get here tonight. Gotta have some respect.'

'Five minutes!'

Ramón, the head of the agency that had employed us for the night, stuck his head round the door, his conspiratorial grin temporarily masking his Neanderthal features: he was all bald head and low brow.

'Guys! Lighten up. It's fucking Christmas Eve. Come on. I want to see some energy this session. *Dale caña.* Give it some welly. And don't drink on stage. The disco owner is already complaining.'

He looked down at me as I huddled on a piece of cardboard on the floor, trying to stop my outfit from getting stained by the peach liqueur that had been kicked over earlier on. One of the disco security guards had already threatened to beat me over the head for breaking the rules: shepherds at the nativity scene weren't meant to knock back shots of Jack Daniels. They weren't meant to be herding goats, either, I thought. But no one had been able to find a sheep in time. So goats was what I had. You could allow for a certain amount of creativity when re-enacting the birth of Christ at an all-night disco on the Spanish coast. It wasn't traditional for the son of God to be surrounded by topless women in red and white furry thongs, either. Nor, come to think of it, could I

282

remember Christmas cards with the Virgin depicted as 'Cyber Mary', whatever that meant. Eventually we'd made Salud a silver dress, with an @ sign as a halo. She wore it with the usual disdain she adopted when having to do disco jobs, but when money was tight it was hard to turn down work.

'And Zine!' Ramón called out above the din leaking through the half-open door. 'Stop dancing like an African tribesman. You're supposed to be a saint. Don't move so much. Just stand there and look holy.'

Zine sniffed and took another drag on his cigarette.

'Cheer up, Darkie,' said Alberto. 'We'll be going home in about five hours.'

'¡Qué fuerte, tío!'

'OK. Next session we're in the back hall, with the Sexómanos. Don't fuck it up. And if they try to get you involved, just go along with it. Carratalá's already on my case.'

We headed down the stairs again for the second set, me carrying a kid under each arm, totally oblivious to the roar of decadent life around them. Something about stepping out from the haze of hashish smoke and muffled music into the explosion of noise that was the disco itself had the effect of waking us up – time to be back on stage and perform. Hardly the West End, but there was still a certain tingle of nerves. One of the goats, I noticed with alarm, had taken an unhealthy interest in my shepherd's costume and was nibbling at the corner of the old sheet I'd used as a robe. I shook its head away as we mounted the stage.

In front of us, on a T section of the platform that extended out among the audience, the Sexómanos were already well into their act. Four topless girls were doing some kind of sex show that involved pulling guys out from the crowd, sitting them down on chairs and then 'performing' – deep throat kissing, stripping, lap dancing, and in some cases engaging in genital contact. Salud had told me about them before with a sneer, but this was the first time I'd actually seen them. Sometimes they got so into their work they dragged people off stage for a proper screw in some back room. Not just girls, either. It would be the boys' turn to do the same with girls from the audience in a few minutes' time.

The 'nativity scene' placed itself behind the sex show as best it could. Zine and Salud stood in the centre, Salud holding a plastic Baby Jesus, while Zine looked on paternally, falling into his role as Christian saint, even blessing the onlookers from time to time with papal gestures of the hand. At the same time the muscle man started doing high kicks and the two top-less Mother Christmases danced suggestively at the sides – a difficult task given the hard-core action occurring in front of them: who could be bothered with abnormally large breasts when the Sexómano girls were caressing shaving foam onto the testicles of one of the punters? Alberto, meanwhile, had got into things with more gusto, and was having his Santa out-fit ripped off him by one of the performers looking for something more interesting than the usual limp, fumbling response she got from the nerds in the crowd. Live sex with a dwarf? I could see how you quickly got jaded with this kind of thing, and I looked down protectively at the goats. They didn't seem too worried, chewing instead on the stick of cane I'd picked up as a makeshift staff. Above us, in a cage hanging from the ceiling, a naked dancer was sliding up and down a pole without using either hands or feet. How *did* she do that?

'*¡Tu puta madre!*' Above the noise came an angry shout. I turned to look and saw Alberto holding a hand to his bleeding nose, swearing at the muscle man, who had now stopped his kicking and was looking concerned and guiltily down at the dwarf. From Salud's gesture with her leg I worked out what had happened: Alberto had been hit in the face by the muscle man's foot. He staggered over towards me at the side of the stage while the rest of them carried on. Pulling him over, I untied the piece of cloth I was using as a belt and handed it to him to wipe his face clean. The bleeding wasn't heavy, but he was shocked.

'Here,' I said, pulling out a miniature whisky bottle I'd picked up in the dressing room. 'Have a slug of this.'

'Prick wasn't looking where he was kicking,' he said, taking a drink. 'I was just getting it together with that girl as well.'

I wiped away some more drops of blood. 'Don't think he's done any damage,' I said. 'Might swell a bit.'

'Nah. I'll be fine,' he said, finishing the whisky. 'Cheers for that.'

'Oi!' There was a crash on the floor between us and we both jumped away. A security guard with a baseball bat in his hands glared at us, biceps bursting out of his overstretched T-shirt. The goats started bleating. 'No fucking drinking.'

Back in the dressing room, we were all silent for a while, a combination of tiredness and a sense of having been sullied by sharing the stage with the sex show. Even the muscle man didn't speak, still ashamed for having kicked Alberto in the face. Alberto just sat and rolled another joint on the floor, pretending nothing had happened. Salud looked over to me with an expression of desperation – I was crouching down by the goats, cleaning up little balls of shit they'd been depositing since we'd got back. I was sure the guard had frightened the hell out of them. The atmosphere seemed abnormally aggressive.

'This place is amazing,' said Zine, a sleepy look on his face as he leaned heavily against the wall. I could tell he didn't want to sit down in case he fell asleep.

'I think your *moro* is freaked out by it all,' said Chelo above the throbbing music.

'No wonder Bin Laden wants to destroy the decadent West,' I said with a grin. Zine looked down and laughed, then closed his eyes.

'*¡Qué fuerte, tío!*'

Lucía called Zine on Salud's mobile phone just before we went out for our final set. It was six in the morning and she was just going to bed. We wouldn't be back in the city for another couple of hours at least. Zine spoke to her while the rest of us got ready for the last appearance. Half drunk and clumsy with tiredness, we looked even more of a sight than before: Chelo had given up on creating a uniform layer of paint over her breasts, which now looked like slightly grubby balloons at the end of a children's birthday party, while Alberto had stripped down to his vest and underpants, the only reminder of who he was supposed to be the pointed Santa hat with its white bobble on his head.

'I'd take this off as well if I could get away with it,' he said. 'I get hotter the later it gets. Here, Princess, have a toke on this.' And he passed the evening's last joint over to Chelo's red-headed colleague. Apart from a pinkness in the skin, you would hardly have known he'd been kicked in the face earlier on.

I decided to leave the goats tied up on an outside balcony near the dressing room this time. They were happy enough there. At this hour in the morning no one would care anyway. It was the dreg end of the night, everyone looking their worst, and civility at its lowest ebb. We'd go down, mix with the people, dance on one of the podiums for a few minutes, then finish as quickly as we could get away with. The most painful bit would come later, when we'd have to wait around for an hour or more to get paid.

Zine passed the phone to me to put away in Salud's bag as we began trudging out the door to head downstairs once again. He seemed moved in some way. 'Lucía,' he said, and smiled.

I put my arm round his shoulders. 'It's time to go.'

Down in the disco, the smell of tobacco and alcohol from spilled drinks mixed with the sweat of over a thousand people jiggling to a monotone rhythm. Make-up on girls' faces was beginning to fade or smear, while the boys' sparkling fashion shirts wilted with the dampness rising from their skin. We pushed our way forward through the crowd, Zine just behind me coming last. From the corner of my eye I could see he was holding his staff more like an outstretched lance.

'Hey! San José!' a group of boys by the bar called out. I laughed. Throughout the night he'd been attracting more attention than even the topless Mother Christmases.

There was a shout and I felt a body shunted hard against me from behind.

'¡Cuidado! Watch out!'

I turned to see what was going on: one of the drunken boys was now looking at us as though wanting a fight, but Zine just gazed at me blankly and walked on, forcing me to continue.

'What happened?'

He said nothing and pushed me forward.

We danced as best we could on the cramped podium. Zine fell back on his cave-man routine, while Alberto waltzed with Chelo, his head bobbing up and down at the level of her belly button. The muscle man had forgotten his shame of earlier and had resorted to his high kicks – the only move in his repertoire – but he aimed them out over the heads of the crowd this time. Salud danced as gracefully as ever under her silver cyber-halo, a serene smile masking an intense desire to get the hell out of there. We were supposed to be at her parents' house for Christmas lunch soon; we'd be lucky if we had time for a shower and a couple of hours' sleep beforehand.

As we danced, I caught sight of two of the bouncers with their baseball bats checking out the entrance on the far side of the hall. In the dim light I thought I could make out broken glass on the floor. People were drifting in and out, cold blasts of winter morning sea air wafted in like welcome slaps in the face. The guards were leaning over one man, who was clearly very frightened, pinning him with their sneers and shaven heads against the doorway.

'I hate this place,' Salud said in my ear as I made to dance with her. I was bored now and tired. It wouldn't be long.

After a signal from Ramón we all stopped and walked off the podium in a line. No one seemed to notice we were no longer there – the eye-candy for drugged, pissed party-goers simply vanishing as though we'd never appeared in the first place. Why did people pay us to do this?

As we headed back to get changed, Zine fell behind. I was tired, otherwise I would have gone back and dragged him along with us, but it was already too late. I reached the stairs back up to the dressing room before I realized what was going on. A girl screamed and when I looked round I noticed that Zine was no longer behind me. Down at the bar the crowd was concentrating on a single space, surging forward towards it. From the left the two bouncers came running through, throwing people out of their way as the moment they'd been waiting for all night finally came: a fight.

I knew that Zine was involved, and that he would be hurt. I ran down and tried to push my way past. In the crush it was impossible to get through: girls were squeezing their way out in fright while boys leant further in to see what was happening. Before I could make any headway I had been tossed to one side by the heaving mass of flesh. There was no way in. I heard Zine shouting as the bouncers reached the middle of the fray, pulling him and his assailant away towards the door and the car park outside, baseball bats high above their heads.

'He's with us,' I shouted desperately, jumping up above a sea of closely cropped heads to make myself heard. 'Leave him alone. He's with the *performance*.'

There was a metallic clang as the door closed behind them. The stuffy air once again, the incessant beat, girls drinking beer from small bottles. The crowd began to disperse: the show was over.

THE BABY

When we asked for Lucía at the hospital reception, an elderly lady wearing a dark-blue cardigan and a silver chain with a cross around her neck came up to talk to us.

'It's terrible,' she whispered, her eyes glistening under the lifeless neon striplights. 'I'm Lucía's aunt. Her mother's with her now.'

She kissed us on the cheeks, stretching up to reach us and feel human warmth, as though desperate for air.

'They're keeping her in intensive care for another day. We thought she might have moved to another ward this afternoon, but they need to keep her under observation. She's very weak. We almost lost her last night.'

Through the open doors came the sound of explosions as the city celebrated the Fallas spring festival – the beginning of new life: cars rolling towards the centre to see the midnight firework spectacle by the river; a hornblast; bats screeching as they hunted for breakfast.

Several floors above us, Lucía was circling in and out of deathly sleep, while in a flat in Casablanca

Zine was sitting by a phone, waiting for news.

It had taken them less than two days to send him back to Morocco, despite the Christmas holidays: a day in a cell, a ride in a police van to Madrid, then a flight back home.

'They treated me fine,' he'd told me over the phone when he got there. 'As I said they would. I even got an in-flight meal.'

It had been the first news we'd had of him. Forcing my way out of the disco, I'd arrived just as the police were driving him away, his face like wax behind the glass of the squad-car window. A couple of local policemen standing on dawn duty at the disco gates had got involved when they saw the bouncers dragging him out from inside, looking as though they were about to beat the hell out of him. They'd stopped his head being broken, but in doing so discovered another illegal immigrant who would now be successfully removed from the country. Just in time to add him to that year's statistics.

No one would give us any information on what had happened to him, though, and it came as a relief when he called. At least we knew he was safe, even if he had been sent back to the 'other side'.

Lucía had cried for over a week.

Since then, over the past months he'd been living with his uncle again, old wounds between them healing, it seemed. We talked on the phone every few weeks. After the initial shock, the plan had been for Lucía to have the child in Spain then head down to Morocco to get married, Zine having finally ceded this was the best plan. They would then return to Valencia with him and the baby when the paperwork was sorted.

I knew Lucía had rung him just before entering

293

hospital. But for twenty-four hours no one had spoken to him. He knew nothing about all of this: someone would have to call.

Lucía's aunt grasped both our hands with a smile sadder than any expression I'd ever seen.

'And the baby?' Salud asked.

She shook her head.

A strangling sensation rose in my throat and I willed myself not to let the tears fall. They'd told us on the phone things had gone wrong, but we'd thought there was still some hope.

We sat down on the hard plastic brown chairs in the entrance hall. On the seat next to me someone had left the morning's paper: the same story that had dominated over the past months: the attack on Iraq was imminent now and would come any day.

Children in pain were crying in corners, tired parents and worried relatives slumped across one another trying to catch some sleep. Others shuffled along in slippers across the shiny floor, sipping at tiny plastic cups of hot strong coffee, eyelids half closed as they prepared for another night waiting for news. Everyone here was on the edge: only the occasional nurse starting a shift seemed anything less than close to breakdown.

Lucía's aunt sat between the two of us, still grasping our hands, the silver crucifix between her breasts quivering as her body trembled very slightly. Salud was using her free hand to clear her eyes, lines of watery black make-up streaming down her cheeks. I stared ahead at the empty walls and the blank shattered people pacing to and fro.

'It was all going very well. They had all the maternity doctors there because there were no other cases to deal with over the weekend. Then – I don't know, it's a bit confusing, ¿sabes? Lucía just started bleeding. She haemorrhaged. The baby was very big, or something. I don't understand. She was three months premature. It was too late for a caesarean – she'd already entered the birth canal. The doctors had to drag her out with forceps in order to save Lucía: they had to open her up to find out where the bleeding was in order to stop it.'

She took her hand away from mine and pulled a white handkerchief from her sleeve. One of the threads from the lace border caught on her ring as she brought it to her face.

'She bled a lot,' she continued. 'They had to give her eight bags of blood. They're not even sure now if she'll . . .'

Salud and I looked at each other as she hesitated for a second, both wanting to say something to reassure her, to tell her Lucía would be all right. But it felt like tempting fate: Lucía was still too close to death for us to make blandly hopeful comments.

'The baby was without oxygen for a long time. She was only just alive when she was finally born, but . . . it didn't take her long to die. The doctors said it was better that way anyway: she would have been a vegetable, and her kidneys didn't function properly. We just have to pray now for Lucía.'

'Can we see her?' Salud asked.

'They only allow one visitor a day in intensive care. Her mother's been staying here, sleeping in the waiting room. The nurses have been very good. No one's known a case like this before – not for forty-three years, I heard one doctor say. I think they've all been very sad over it.'

Lucía's father came out into the hall and walked towards us. Again the smile I had seen a few minutes earlier on his sister's face. I felt ashamed of barely being able to control my own emotions – it was his granddaughter who had died and his daughter who was now critically ill.

We spoke a little about the situation, and he repeated much of what Lucía's aunt had already said. He seemed keen for us not to worry too much, soothing our anguish. It should have been us in that position, I thought, but the tragedy seemed to have brought out a deeply human side in him. In the haze of grief, I even remember us all laughing at some point at some light-hearted comment he made. He was tired, and was just heading off back home for a shower before returning to the hospital to spend another night.

He put his arm around my shoulders as we walked towards the door.

'Could I ask you a favour?' he said.

Back home I dialled a Casablanca number, a strange nervous current running through me as I pressed each button. With a click someone picked up the phone at the other end and there came the hissing sound of a long-distance call.

'*Halo?*'

'Zine,' I said. 'It's me.'

CASABLANCA

'*T*hat's where the bomb was,' the taxi driver said as we jerked from side to side amid the late-night traffic. 'Hotel Farah.'

The building was cordoned off, policemen standing at the doorway now that the glass and body parts had been cleaned up, chipboard replacing the windows.

'Looks better like this,' he grinned.

It was an ugly, modern hotel, only now it was famous for being the site of the bloodiest of the terrorist bombings that had taken place in the city when suicide squads had struck three days earlier. The war in Iraq had officially come to an end, but the violence continued. Now Morocco was the latest target for blind intolerance and hate.

On the pavements, girls in jeans and revealing tops walked in pairs or with groups of male and female friends under the porticoes of the dusty Art Deco blocks that made up the city centre. A light cool breeze blew in off the Atlantic, the sounds of discos shouting in waves through my open window as salmon-pink street lights flashed overhead. From the port came the smell of fish on the turn, blending with the petrol fumes of the boys in new BMWs and Volkswagens cruising past us as they squeezed down the middle of the street, oblivious to the lines dividing one side from the other. There was little to differentiate this city from a Spanish town, or a city on the French Mediterranean: the buildings, the cars, the clothes, the heat, even the palm trees. It was all very familiar. The distinction came in small things: an extra layer of dust, perhaps; the occasional sight of men in traditional dress; a very slightly darker hue to the skin – but only when viewed as a whole: there were plenty of paler faces among the crowds; the slowness of the driving, not the usual squealing of tyres as the lights turned green; the sight of minarets pushing upwards from the modern city below. Casablanca was what Seville or Malaga might have been like had the Moors never been expelled from Spain. It was vibrant and fun, and now it was organizing itself to express its rejection of the suicide bombings: people sending text messages of solidarity to one another, setting up protest sit-ins, or demonstrations for the following weekend. The Hand of Fatima, which I had seen all over Spain and Portugal on my trip, usually on doors as an ancient Moorish charm to ward off the evil eye, was here being used as a symbol for the anti-terror movement.

Zine had arranged for us to meet at a Spanish restaurant in the centre. It would be better that way, he said; inviting me to his uncle's house could prove difficult. Outside, two security guards in black were standing at the door, preventing cars from parking on the stretch in front of the restaurant for fear of car-bombs. I'd already seen the same at a dozen hotels and 'Western' venues along the way. How quickly things changed, and how great the effect a small group of people creating fear could have.

The back wall was covered with a giant screen showing footage from bullfights, with a backing track of Mexican pop music.

Zine didn't get up from his table when he saw me, simply waving with a guarded smile. We shook hands as I sat down. Normally we would probably have kissed one another on the cheeks. Time had changed things. I would have travelled earlier to see him but for the strong feeling I got in the weeks after the baby's death that I would have been unwelcome. He needed to grieve on his own.

'It's good to see you,' he said. His voice was heavy.

He'd let his hair grow again – not quite as long as when I'd first met him on the farm, but the ringlets were beginning to cascade over the tops of his ears again.

I put my hand on his arm. 'I'm very sorry about what happened.'

'Of course. It is very sad. But . . .' He paused for a second. The waiter came over and we ordered some wine with anchovies in vinegar. A style of food originally taken to Spain by the Moors was now offered as a typically Spanish dish in Morocco.

We talked a little about my trip over, about how hot it was for me, what I'd seen of the city. Chit-chat just to try to connect once again, but what I wanted to ask, the reason I was there, could not be ignored, blocking everything else from view.

'How's Lucía?' he asked.

I knew they talked often on the phone; he probably knew better than I what she had been going through, but I'd had the chance at least to see her. Only a couple of nights previously she'd broken down at a bar Salud and I had taken her to for dinner. The sight of her once-cheerful face collapsing in sobs on seeing a new-born baby with the family at the next table still played on my mind.

'Sometimes I'm amazed at how well she seems to be getting on, then other times it shows,' I said. 'She still looks pale, especially in the evenings, but her parents have been with her most of the time, and she's already beginning to get back into her theatre life: they're planning a new show for the end of the summer, as you probably know. I think she'll be well enough by then. It's important for her.'

For Zine to return to Spain now was out of the question, but at no point talking to either of them over the previous months had I got the impression that Lucía might travel to Morocco to see him yet. I hadn't asked why, but I had the sense that the relationship was in a state of flux, neither perhaps knowing for sure whether to carry on or finish it: the stress of what they'd been through could either bring them closer together or separate them for good.

'How are you?' I asked.

He placed his elbows on the table, holding the weight of his head by the temples, lids drooping slightly over tired eyes.

'I don't think about it much,' he said after a pause. 'It seems hardly true. I start feeling guilty – about how I'm taken up with life here, not thinking about the baby. All I cared about was Lucía. Now I think I should have felt sadder about my daughter.'

He stuck a toothpick in one end of a whitened anchovy on the plate then folded it, spiked it again at the other end and placed it in his mouth. In the

301

semi-darkness of the restaurant it seemed his posture had changed since Spain – a roundness in the shoulders, his head jutting forwards slightly.

'For a while I just wanted to get away. People always asking. Now they don't – you just get on with things. But now you're here and . . . This is the first time I've spoken about it for weeks. It makes me sad.'

On the giant screen the programme had changed to a live Spanish football match being shown on local TV – Valencia were losing at home to Real Madrid. A bald, brown-skinned man with sticking-out front teeth had taken off his shirt after scoring and was running with his arms stretched out, pretending to glide like a bird.

'But how long ago was it?' Zine went on. 'Two months? Seems like much, much longer. For a while there were all kinds of things I thought would be closed off to me once the baby came, even though I'm here and she's – she was – there. Then you start thinking: I can go back and enjoy all those things again. But you don't really feel like it, you don't want to.'

I poured him some more wine and he lit a cigarette.

'It was a beautiful experience – the pregnancy, I remember that. Lucía says we could try again. But . . .'

'Do you want to?'

He shrugged.

'Have you spoken to her recently?' I asked.

'We call each other.'

'Would it frighten you, going through it all again?'

'It wouldn't be the same.'

The rest of the food came and we ate in silence. I ordered another bottle of wine. The intensity he had always had was still there, but some of the electricity that had seemed to flow constantly around him had dulled slightly. It was difficult to tell, though: perhaps my perception was obscured by the darkness, the noise, my own expectation that the experience must have changed him in some deep way. I'd been moved by it myself, visiting Lucía in hospital, then following her progress as she mended herself and started getting back into work. But sometimes people just carried on the same.

'I want you to take something back to Lucía for me,' he said as we finished eating. Putting his hand into a jacket pocket, he pulled out an object wrapped in brown tissue paper. 'Here, I'll show you.'

He pulled the layers off and placed a little crafted ball of brass in my hand, its surface marked by tiny dents. At the top there was a little star-shaped button. From the feel of it, it was hollow, but it felt good in my hand: warm; something you wanted to handle and caress, perhaps absent-mindedly while thinking or talking to someone.

'It's an orange,' he said without further explanation.

I wrapped it again and put it carefully in my bag, puzzled, but with something of an idea of its meaning: an orange, an ancient Arabic symbol of love, the union of two souls. I would take it to Lucía as soon as I got back.

'I'm working with my uncle now,' he said. I knew this from our phone conversations. Before he'd given the impression he'd been running away from precisely this: his uncle's little import and export business, and the hostility of his competitive elder cousins. A family where he felt a stranger: a reminder of the loss of his own parents.

'How does it suit you?' I asked.

'Well,' he said, 'bad things never last a hundred years.'

An ironic glint lit up his eyes for a second. It was the phrase Lucía had used the night they met in Valencia. We both sniggered, almost cautiously at first, but slowly building up until eventually we were both laughing out loud, the tension between us easing and slipping away like dead skin. I was pleased for him. Something, at least, was going right.

'You old bastard,' I said.

'What?' he asked with a smile.

'All that effort to find you a bloody job on a farm.'

'So? You were going that way anyway, no?'

'Yes, but I'd planned on going alone.'

'How can you travel around Moorish Spain without a Moor?'

I shrugged.

'It was fate. Otherwise you wouldn't have found all those jewels you kept talking about. You needed me to help you see.'

We left the restaurant and caught a red 'small-taxi' to the Corniche, with its hotels, nightclubs and low white villas: a cross between Los Angeles and the hill-top Moorish villages of Andalusia we'd been driving around only six months before. Satellite dishes the size of bathtubs sat on every roof, like inert sunbathers trying to catch burning rays, while in the distance the gigantic modern mosque of Hassan II perched on the sea's edge, the most westerly point of Islam. Its minaret was a thick square tower over two hundred metres high, the younger and larger brother of the Almohad minarets of the Kutubiyya in Marrakesh and La Giralda in Seville. The old lighthouse to its left whipped out beams of light above our heads, catching the milky haze blowing in off the ocean, while waves rippled onto the beach like cream. After the recent bombings, going dancing and drinking here felt something like a political statement.

'And your hunt for Musa's treasure?' Zine asked with a smile. 'You've found it all now? The secret jewels?' Despite his grief, he still remembered the point of my journey, how all of this began.

'I think there's more to be discovered,' I said. 'But it may be increasingly hard to find.'

There was something of a ghostly presence to Al-Andalus, I'd realized: a spirit which had entered Spain with the Moors and which perhaps had never left, disguising itself to remain safe from harm when the world had turned against it. It was easy to imagine that some kind of spell, as in the legend, had been cast over it as a form of protection. To say I had finally discovered its secrets felt almost irreverent, like claiming to have found the Philosopher's Stone. Moorish Spain may have functioned as some kind of alchemist's crucible on one level, yet as I had seen from the people I'd met on my journey, it could mean different things depending on who you were. My friend Pedro and Camilo had studied Arabic together, yet had come away with contrasting ideas about the Arab legacy; and neither of them would have much in common with Muhammad the convert in Granada. Perhaps only the prince came truly close to living in 'Moorish Spain': for him it was less about ideas and theories and more something he experienced every day.

The secret legacy of Al-Andalus – Musa's treasure – seemed to be disguised and half forgotten, yet it was a symbol of hope that something of another time had survived – a time when Muslims, Jews and Christians had shared the same 'spiritual space', in Burckhardt's phrase. Difficult to perceive, perhaps, but a channel, a current still present nonetheless: something to tap into, like an underground river beneath a desert. Dig around and you might find traces of it. In some places, I suspected, it came close to the surface of its own accord. Ignored and unrecognized, however, my fear was that it might be gradually running dry, perhaps disappearing for good.

In going out and looking for Musa's treasure, I'd made a more personal discovery as well, though: a deeper understanding of Spain, perhaps, which, although it could never remove the fact that I was a foreigner there, at least made the country less foreign to me. Concepts such as 'home', I was beginning to think, were perhaps less important than I'd imagined: Spain had once been home to Moors and Jews, yet they had been forced to convert or leave. Homes could be unstable places, and putting too much emphasis on finding one was probably a mistake. Things changed. One minute you might be settling down, a baby on the way, the next it was all gone.

Tankers were lining up on the horizon to enter Casablanca port, like little bunches of glow-worms in the night. Despite the darkness and thick salty air, you sensed the openness and vastness of the ocean at your side here: inviting and forbidding; a barrier and a gateway to other worlds.

Zine put his arm through mine as we walked along the pavement, past palm trees and pretty girls charged with sexual energy, black tresses flowing down their backs like velvet. It was so different from what I remembered of Egypt, where more and more women covered their hair in veils, arranging them in such a way that their golden earrings just poked out from underneath the wrapping. There I'd sensed a constant unease and anger: about the first war in the Gulf, about the Palestinians, about the West, about the overbearing power of the ruling party and the danger of extremists. Pseudo-Islamic conformity was imposed through fear. Here it still felt a world away from all of that, despite the bombing. Fundamentalists, with their bland uniform of square beard, short hair and humourless expressions, were far less in evidence. Nor did Moroccan men walk around with fake bruises on their foreheads from praying, like many Egyptians did as a kind of badge of holiness. You had to pinch yourself to remember the violence of just a few days before. There was so much joy of life here, something I'd always found and admired among the Spanish. And of course the city still had a Spanish name. For a moment it was hard to tell if the place felt like an Arab version of Spain, or if Spain were a European version of Morocco. Although, of course, once upon a time there hadn't been such a distinction.

'What will you do?' I asked Zine as we stopped to look out at the sea. A group of skinny boys in shorts were playing football on the beach, their bodies bending and twisting like rubber as they reached and curled for the ball.

'I'll work with my uncle for a while, then see what happens.'

'And Lucía?'

The waves sighed as they spilled themselves onto the land. Above our heads a seagull hovered motionless and silent, held still by a momentary current of air blowing in off the sea.

There was no reply.

GLOSSARY

Al-Andalus Name used by the Moors at any one time for the areas of the Iberian peninsula under their control

Almohads Fundamentalist warrior monks who took over Morocco and Al-Andalus during the twelfth century; successors of the Almoravids

Almoravids Fundamentalist warrior monks who took over Morocco and Al-Andalus in the eleventh century; eventually defeated by the Almohads

Andalusia Southern region of modern Spain; name derives from Al-Andalus

Caliph Religious and often political head of the world Islamic community; compares with emir, a purely political title meaning 'ruler'

Ferdinand & Isabel Named 'the Catholic Kings' for their conquest of Muslim-held Granada; their marriage united the kingdoms of Castille and Aragon; instigators of the Spanish Inquisition

Judería   Old Jewish quarter of a Spanish town

Marrano   Derogative name given to the Jewish community in Christian-held areas of Spain; translates as 'dirty swine'

Mihrab   Niche in the inner wall of a mosque indicating the direction of prayer

Morisco   Derogative name given to the Moors of Spain after the fall of Granada in 1492; literally 'little Moor'

Moro   Spanish for 'Moor'

Mouro   Portuguese for 'Moor'

Mozarabs   Arabized Christians living in Moorish-controlled areas; literally 'would-be Arabs'

Mudejars   Moors who remained in territories conquered by the Christians; term usually refers to the period before 1492 (cf. Moriscos)

Musa   The Arab governor of North Africa who followed Tariq in his invasion of Spain in 712

Nasrids   Ruling dynasty of Granada from the thirteenth century till 1492

Palo   Particular song or style of music within flamenco

Reconquest   Term usually applied to any Christian conquest of Moorish-held territory

Saeta	Haunting song performed at religious ceremonies, usually in Andalusia
Santiago	St James; patron saint of Spain, nick-named Matamoros: the Moor-slayer
Tablao	Bar or restaurant where flamenco is regularly performed
Taifas	Period of 'petty kingdoms' into which Al-Andalus split up after the fall of the Córdoba caliphate in 1031; ended with the arrival of the Almoravids
Tariq	The first Muslim invader to cross into Spain, in 711; Gibraltar is named after him (*jabal Tariq* – the mountain of Tariq)
Umayyads	Ruling dynasty in Al-Andalus from 756 to 1031
Visigoths	Rulers of the Iberian Peninsula at the time of the Moorish conquest

ANDALUS TIMELINE

Fifth century AD	Visigoths begin conquest of Iberian Peninsula
622	Beginning of the Islamic era
632	Muhammad dies
711	First Muslim armies led by Tariq land in Spain
712	Musa arrives in Spain to take part in conquest
722	Battle of Covadonga in Asturias, northern Spain; the traditional date for the start of the 'Reconquest'
732	Battle of Poitiers in France: furthest extension of Moorish advance
756	Abd al-Rahman I becomes emir of the politically independent Islamic realm of Al Andalus
929	Abd al-Rahman III declares himself 'caliph'; Moorish Golden Age begins
1031	Córdoba caliphate ends; Moorish Spain breaks up into *taifa* (little kingdoms)
1085	Christian King Alfonso VI conquers Toledo
1094	El Cid takes control of Valencia

1080s–1140s	Almoravids take control of Al-Andalus
Early 1100s	School of Translators established in Toledo
1126	Averroes born in Córdoba (dies 1196 in Marrakesh)
1135	Maimonides born in Córdoba (dies 1204 in Cairo)
1140s–1220s	Almohads control Al-Andalus
1147	The Second Crusade gets side-tracked by the Christian conquest of Lisbon
1165	Ibn al-Arabi born in Murcia (dies 1240 in Damascus)
1212	Battle of Las Navas de Tolosa: major Christian victory
1232	Nasrid dynasty begins reign over Granada
1236	Christian King Ferdinand III conquers Córdoba
1238	Christian King James I 'the Conqueror' takes Valencia
1248	Ferdinand conquers Seville
1391	First big pogroms against the Jewish community in Christian-held territory
1479	Castille and Aragon unite
1481	Inquisition set up
1492	Granada falls; Jews expelled from Spain; Columbus discovers America
1526	Moors (now called Moriscos) forced to convert and banned from reading and writing Arabic

DUENDE
Jason Webster

'I FOUND HIS DESCRIPTIONS OF THE FLAMENCO
UNDERWORLD IRRESISTIBLE . . . I COULDN'T PUT IT DOWN'
Chris Stewart, author of *Driving Over Lemons*

When Jason Webster heads off for Spain in search of *duende*, the
intense emotional state – part ecstasy, part desperation – so
intrinsic to flamenco, he has no idea what to expect.

What he finds is a kaleidoscope of experience and excitement:
From the tyranny of his guitar teacher, practising for hours on end
until his fingers bleed to his passionate affair with Lola, a
flamenco dancer (and older woman) married to the gun-toting
Vicente, which causes him to flee Alicante in fear of his life. In
Madrid, he falls in with Gypsies and meets the imperious Jesús.
Joining their dislocated, cocaine-fuelled world, stealing cars by
night and sleeping away the days in tawdry rooms, he finds
himself spiralling self-destructively downwards. It is only when
he arrives in Granada bruised and battered, after two years total
immersion in the flamenco lifestyle that he is able to put his
obsession into context.

'FASCINATING . . . THE BEST TRAVEL WRITING IS NOT
ABOUT TOPOGRAPHY BUT PEOPLE, AND WEBSTER'S
INFILTRATION OF THIS NOTORIOUSLY CLOSED COMMUNITY
MAKES FOR COMPULSIVE READING . . . WEBSTER IS AN
EXCEPTIONAL WRITER, AND THIS IS A GREAT BOOK'
Guardian

'THE AUTOBIOGRAPHY-AS-TRAVELOGUE THAT IS ALSO A
RITE OF PASSAGE IS A FORM WHICH WORKED BRILLIANTLY
FOR LAURIE LEE AND BRUCE CHATWIN – BOTH NOVELISTS
AS WELL AS SEEKERS AFTER THE TRUTH-BEHIND-THE-
TRUTH. LADIES AND GENTLEMEN, WE HAVE A NEW STAR
OF THE GENRE: JASON WEBSTER'
Daily Mail

0 552 99997 0

BLACK SWAN

A SELECTED LIST OF TRAVEL WRITING
AVAILABLE FROM TRANSWORLD PUBLISHERS

81341 2	LIFE IN A POSTCARD	Rosemary Bailey	£7.99
99806 0	NEITHER HERE NOR THERE	Bill Bryson	£7.99
77157 0	A WOLVERINE IS EATING MY LEG	Tim Cahill	£7.99
77120 1	THE CLOUD GARDEN	Tom Hart Dyke and Paul Winder	£7.99
81479 6	FRENCH SPIRITS	Jeffrey Greene	£6.99
77098 1	GETTING TO MANANA	Miranda Innes	£6.99
81613 6	A YEAR OF RUSSIAN FEASTS	Catherine Cheremeteff Jones	£6.99
14595 5	BETWEEN EXTREMES	Brian Keenan and John McCarthy	£7.99
81490 7	BEST FOOT FORWARD	Susie Kelly	£6.99
99967 9	A GHOST UPON YOUR PATH	John McCarthy	£7.99
81601 2	HOLY COW!	Sarah Macdonald	£6.99
99841 9	NOTES FROM AN ITALIAN GARDEN	Joan Marble	£7.99
77108 2	NOTES FROM A ROMAN TERRACE	Joan Marble	£7.99
81250 5	BELLA TUSCANY	Frances Mayes	£6.99
81635 7	MONSOON DIARY	Shoba Narayan	£7.99
81602 0	ALL THE RIGHT PLACES	Brad Newsham	£6.99
81550 4	FOUR CORNERS	Kira Salak	£7.99
81566 0	FROM HERE YOU CAN'T SEE PARIS	Michael Sanders	£7.99
81584 9	WITHOUT RESERVATIONS: THE TRAVELS OF AN INDEPENDENT WOMAN	Alice Steinbach	£6.99
99928 8	INSTRUCTIONS FOR VISITORS	Helen Stevenson	£6.99
81555 5	AN EMBARRASSMENT OF MANGOES	Ann Vanderhoof	£7.99
99997 0	DUENDE	Jason Webster	£7.99